—The
Influen
Manager

The Influential Manager

HOW TO DEVELOP A POWERFUL MANAGEMENT STYLE

LEE BRYCE

PIATKUS

First published in 1991 by
Judy Piatkus (Publishers) Ltd of
5 Windmill Street, London W1P 1HF

First paperback edition 1994

The moral right of the author has been asserted

*A catalogue record for this book is
available from the British Library*

ISBN 0–7499–1083–6 (Hbk)

ISBN 0–7499–1357–6 (Pbk)

Edited by Carol Franklin
Designed by Paul Saunders

Typeset in 11/13pt Linotron Plantin Light by
Computerset, Harmondsworth, Middx.
Printed and bound in Great Britain by
Butler & Tanner Ltd, Frome

CONTENTS

1   There are Many Ways of Being Influential   1

2   What is Power?   15

3   What is Influence?   32

4   Making Yourself Powerful   55

5   Establishing Power When You're New to a Job   76

6   Influencing Your Boss   88

7   Influencing at Meetings   104

8   Using Power to Empower Others   123

9   Developing Personal Power   138

10   How to Lose Gracefully   159

11   Developing a Powerful Image   169

12   Influencing Other Departments   182

13   Watching Out for Dirty Politics   193

References   208

Useful Addresses   209

Recommended Reading   210

Index   211

CHAPTER · 1

THERE ARE MANY WAYS OF BEING INFLUENTIAL

This book is for all managers and aspiring managers who want to get on, become influential and rise up the ladder. It's for everyone who is beginning to realise that being effective is not just about high performance, it is also about being political. Some of you may have come to this conclusion without knowing what to do about it. Or you may be turned off by the machiavellian and underhand nature of the politics you see being practised by some of the people you encounter in business. Much of the currently available advice on how to be influential is superficial and devious. If you feel that this kind of approach is distasteful then this is the book for you.

This is not a superficial book on how to be a super creep, or how to be manipulatively political. The advice you will find in these pages will warn you against using self-seeking power plays which endanger both your position and your friendships. It is based on a sound understanding of human psychology and organisational politics and includes:

- how to play office politics *constructively*;
- how to become a powerful person at work without squashing all the other rats in the rat race;
- how to develop an understanding of human nature, your own personality and behaviour (and other people's), and how to use this knowledge to become more influential; and
- how to use your power and influence to empower other people and so become a first-class manager.

You will find plenty of practical tips on mastering the art of company politics and using your influence to make you an effective manager. You will be encouraged to see power, influence and internal politics as

1

legitimate methods for increasing your worth to your organisation, and speeding up your rise to attaining better and better jobs. You will see how ignoring this aspect of your development will hold you back in your career.

The book is full of advice from managers who have themselves made it into senior jobs in a number of different organisations. I would like to thank them for their time and patience in providing me with a lot of excellent material. The interesting thing about these managers is that they did not all start off with the same advantages, nor did they all follow the same route to success. There is hope for us all. Don't imagine that just because you don't have a degree or the right contacts or accent that you won't make it. Some of the interviewees did start from fairly privileged positions, but not all of them by any means. Three of the successful managers interviewed for the book do not have university degrees, and one of them started his career as a head waiter. Several started off in technical jobs, of the sort that do not classically lead to top positions, for example a computer programmer, journalist, production engineer and a chemist. The one thing that they did have in common was that they all realised early on that they needed to be *political* to get on and get things done.

But, although these managers are all political, they are not all political in the same way. Their styles differ dramatically, in keeping with their personalities and their preferences. Some are tough but charismatic, while others are more low key and influential. Some are confrontational and courageous about taking unpopular decisions, while others have learnt to work their way around problems and to negotiate. Some are urbane, understated and socially sophisticated, while others are energetic, enthusiastic and visionary. The inspiring thing is that all styles can work perfectly well, as long as they fit in with your personality and the culture of your organisation.

PROFILES OF SUCCESS

Here is a short profile of the managers interviewed for the book.

Greg Dyke is a strong, charismatic, high energy person who has enjoyed a spectacular rise to power in the television world. Greg is certainly tough and hard hitting, and is able to take difficult decisions and live with any consequent unpopularity. However his charm, attentiveness to and interest in people wins him a lot of friends. He left school at 18 and was a local newspaper reporter until the age of 24 when he studied politics at York University. He went back to journalism for a short time after university, but wasn't satisfied with the easy slick solutions in that profession. In 1975 he joined Wandsworth Council for community relations and also became active in politics. In 1977 he stood as a Labour candidate for the GLC, but lost the election. Later that year he started his television career by joining London Weekend Television as a researcher for *The London Programme*. He then got more and more responsible jobs in television until 1984 when he was given his big opportunity to put *TV-am* back on to its feet. Greg took this programme, which had made a disastrous start, and made it a success. He increased the revenue for an average hour from £200,000 to £1.7 million. After that success he became the director of programmes for TVS. In 1987 he went back to London Weekend as a director of programmes and then became deputy managing director. He went to Harvard Business School for three months and then returned to take up his current job as managing director of London Weekend Television in March 1990.

Jerry Stockbridge has spent his whole working life in what was part of the Post Office and is now British Telecom. Because of the size of this organisation he has had a varied and demanding career. Jerry worked his way up to a senior position in British Telecom, where he is now in the business communications division as director of the Asia Pacific region. He is an informal, relaxed person and an excellent story-teller. He has made a lot of friends at BT because of his approachable, down-to-earth style. Jerry is no creep. He turns his nose up at a lot of the status symbols that attract other successful managers. He has been known to leave important high-level meetings at half-past five because his son wanted him to watch him play in a school football match. Recently he disconcerted some senior colleagues by insisting on spending a few days in a telephone shop working as a sales assistant. On the other hand, Jerry is a very helpful person who puts himself out for other people. This, plus being good at his job, has enabled him to do well in spite of being a nonconformist at times.

Jerry joined the Post Office after school, in 1962, and was put on a five-year graduate engineering scheme. He became a chartered engineer and also did a post-graduate course in acoustics, but decided instead that he wanted to go into management. He identified a career goal – to become a general manager of a telephone area – and worked out a route for getting there. He spent the next part of his career influencing people in the Post Office to give him the opportunities he needed. He succeeded. In 1979, at the age of 35, Jerry became the general manager of the West London telephone area, thus realising his life's ambition.

BT was changing from state to private sector, and managerially these were difficult times. From 1984 to 1988 Jerry had four different head office jobs and got frustrated with constantly having to build new teams. The reorganisations in BT at this time were disempowering everyone.

In 1988 Jerry took up the opportunity to become director of telecommunications for BT International. This was a pioneering job in which Jerry had to create new business overseas. He manages all overseas contracts except those in the US and Europe. BT continues to change and reorganise and Jerry has become director of the Asia Pacific region. Only people who can cope with change and variety can do well in BT.

Roger French has been a management consultant for most of his working life. He is now the director of corporate development with Coopers and Lybrand's European firm. Coopers merged with Deloittes, Haskins and Sells in 1990 in various countries, including the UK, to become one of the largest auditing and management consultancy practices in the country and in Europe. Roger is the number two in Europe in the merged giant's European executive office.

After studying physics at Oxford Roger spent six years at IBM as a systems engineer. He then spent a further six years at Robson Morrow as a management consultant where he consulted at Marks and Spencer, Lloyd's of London and Woolworths, South Africa. He then became the managing director of the commercial division of a financial conglomerate in South Africa. In 1976 he joined Deloittes in South Africa and built up their South African management consultancy practice from four to thirty people. In 1981 he returned to the UK, as director responsible for Deloittes International. From 1984 to 1988 Roger was the partner responsible for management consulting at the headquarters executive office of Deloittes, Haskins and Sells International in New York. In 1988 he became director of management consulting for Deloittes Europe and continued with the European work when Coopers merged with Deloittes in 1990.

Roger is a very urbane, amusing man with a good brain. His talent for making friends and influencing people from many different cultures has stood him in good stead in his international career. Roger is an example of someone who prefers to be influential rather than powerful. He is very

4

strategic about building alliances and working his way around problems.

Michael Lainas has built a broad-based career, spanning engineering, project management, consultancy, general management and, finally, marketing consultancy. Michael is an open, gregarious person with a hands-on style of management. He is an example of a manager who understands and accepts the role of politics and power, but who is nice rather than machiavellian about it. He understands the value of rapport and friendships, and devotes a lot of time to building good relationships.

His first job was at Plesseys where he qualified as a chartered production engineer. He then spent twelve interesting months in Geneva working for IOS, the unit trust company set up by Bernie Cornfield. Michael was made redundant when IOS went into a major decline, so he moved to ICL to set up an organisation and methods department. This was his first management job and he threw himself enthusiastically into learning about management.

He then established an internal consultancy department for Fitch Lovell, a major food group. During this period he decided that he wanted to move into general management, but couldn't easily do so as an engineer in a food group, so he started to plan his career to achieve his goal. He decided to join an engineering-based organisation where, as a qualified engineer, he would have more credibility to move into general management. He joined the Rank Organisation as a consultant and soon moved into general management.

Michael's first board-level appointment was at Dixons, where he was a director of the retail company for four and a half years. It was an exciting time of dramatic growth. His next step was to become the managing director of Mastercare (the service organisation for Curry's). He was given the brief to expand the company and it doubled its turnover in three years. In search of a new challenge he decided at the age of 39 to do something different.

He joined a dynamic marketing consultancy called Marketing Solutions. Within three months he was on the board, and then became managing director. Michael left Marketing Solutions in 1988 to become the chairman and chief executive of a major division of Holmes and Marchant, a publicly quoted group of marketing agencies. Wanting to run his own business he decided to move to his present position, where he is a shareholder and managing director of a marketing communications agency called Hobson Bayntun.

Keith Manning is the director of strategy and planning at Bull HN Ltd. They are a subsidiary of Bull, a company owned largely by the French government. Bull merged with part of Honeywell (the computer company) in the 1980s. Keith is a very popular manager at Bull. He is a good example of a manager who is able to be nice *and* successful and political at the same time. He is warm, supportive and a good manager of people, yet he is courageous in standing up for what he thinks is right. When he has decided, after careful reflection, that he needs to take action, he takes it and faces up to the consequences. Keith is now on the management committee of the company.

Keith was born in Yorkshire. He graduated in maths from Nottingham University and then in 1965 became a programmer on the sales side at Elliott Automation. Elliott was bought by English Electric which merged with ICT to form ICL. Keith found ICL to be too much like the civil service, so he looked for a faster moving company and joined Honeywell in 1968. He has been with Honeywell ever since, although it has changed hands and names since then. Keith regrets not having moved around some more when he was younger.

Keith joined Honeywell as a salesman in West Yorkshire where he sold computers to anyone he could find. He became an account manager and had to learn to deal with some tough clients. He was successful because he learnt always to give the customer sound advice, the sort Keith would want if he were in his customer's shoes. He became a sales manager and then branch manager in Leeds. In 1980 he moved to London to become the director of product marketing for the data processing division. In 1983 he became the regional sales director for London and the South East.

His present job, which began in 1989, as director of strategy and planning involves him in the front end of marketing. Keith looks at the potential markets and decides which of them Bull should operate in, and how much resource should be applied. He then builds the budget which the operating units use to manage their businesses.

The information technology industry is very fast changing at present, and in many ways this is the most interesting and challenging job of Keith's career. In spite of the challenge of his current job, Keith, as a people person, still hankers after the buzz he used to get from being with the customer.

Martin Smith is an Oxford physics graduate. A witty, bright, charming man, he has been very good at getting sponsors and building an extensive network of contacts. His working career began in 1964 when he joined Arthur Guinness Son and Company in Dublin on their industrial training programme. In 1969 he got an MBA and an MA in economics from Stanford University, California, and returned to the UK to join McKinsey, the management consultants. At McKinsey he worked in the industrial and financial sectors and became a junior engagement manager. This set the pattern for the rest of his career, because he has worked in the financial sector ever since.

Martin joined Citibank in 1973 to run their venture capital subsidiary in London. Then he became the director of corporate finance for Citicorp International Bank Ltd – a merchant bank owned by Citibank. In 1980 he was headhunted to become chairman of Bankers Trust International, which was the merchant banking wing of Bankers Trust in London.

In 1983 Martin left Bankers Trust and joined an old friend, John Craven, one of London's leading financiers, who had recently formed Phoenix Securities. Martin was the third partner to join this corporate finance advisory business. The firm first became established in the City as a consequence of the 'Big Bang' in the securities industry, where they advised over twenty member firms of the London Stock Exchange on the sales of their businesses. Phoenix then developed into a specialist firm advising on mergers and acquisitions in the financial sector world-wide. In 1987, in order to acquire the services of John Craven as chief executive, Morgan Grenfell made an offer for Phoenix which the partners decided to accept. For the next three years, Martin worked as a senior executive in what had become a wholly owned subsidiary of Morgan Grenfell. In June 1990, following the acquisition of Morgan Grenfell by Deutsche Bank, Martin and his partners repurchased Phoenix Securities and are now on their own again. In December 1990 Phoenix admitted Mitsubishi Corporation as a 20 per cent limited partner.

Martin also has another role which is as the chairman of the board of trustees of the Orchestra of the Age of Enlightenment – the leading early music orchestra in London.

Tony Hughes is the service standards director for the restaurant division of Whitbread. Tony radiates warmth, energy and personal power. He is a man of ideas and vision, who inspires his colleagues with his enthusiasm and commitment. Often, when a person has very strong values and wears his heart on his sleeve he commits political suicide by getting up people's noses and being unstrategic. Not so with Tony. He understands that to realise his visions he needs to be political, and that is why he is successful.

He came up through a very different route to many managers. He did not go to university, in fact he left school at 16 and went to a catering college in Manchester. In 1966 he went to Bermuda to work as a head waiter in a hotel. He returned to England in 1968 and became a waiter for Stanneylands, a company owning thirty restaurants and hotels. He became a manager with this group and spent a year opening up new places.

In 1971 he started his long career at Whitbread as a catering manager for pubs and steakhouses. He moved around and upwards in Whitbread and was frequently responsible for opening new catering establishments. During one period in the early 1980s, when he was operations director with Beefeater, they opened a new steakhouse every eight days for two years.

In 1985 Tony spotted TGI Fridays in the US and was very impressed, both with their performance and their management philosophy. TGI Fridays is a lively theme restaurant and bar with an appeal for younger people. He then did what he excelled at; he persuaded Whitbread to go along with his vision, and he managed the hugely successful introduction of TGI Fridays into the UK. Because of what he did with TGI Fridays he was given a job to transfer the best practices from Fridays into the rest of Whitbread's restaurant business. He had achieved a level of service in Fridays not seen in Whitbread before. So now he is the service standards director for Whitbread's restaurant division.

Mike Dearden got a degree in chemistry at Oxford, then joined Distillers in 1964 as a chemistry graduate doing market research. BP bought the chemistry business from Distillers, so he carried on and worked for BP. It was the sort of place where if you kept your nose clean you would have a respectable career, but things moved too slowly, so he lost patience and left. In 1970 he joined Steetly, in Nottinghamshire, as a divisional marketing manager. This was a company with strong family shareholdings. Mike noticed that if you crossed the family you got fired, so he decided to get out first, and joined Philblack in Bristol as a deputy general sales manager. This company was soon acquired by a US oil multinational, so he joined PA Consulting Group as a marketing consultant. He decided that working for PA was a worthwhile alternative to going to business school. It was intellectually very challenging, and he loved consulting, but when he found that, after seven years, moving upwards meant running a consultancy instead of doing his own consulting, he decided to return to industry.

In 1980 Mike joined Castrol Ltd as their international marketing manager. He had no line authority in this first job with Castrol, but it gave him a good opportunity to find his way around the organisation. By this time Mike had become very experienced at marketing and he combined this with an ability to build contacts and a good political sense to do well in Castrol. In 1988 he joined the board as the director of the western hemisphere (South America and Canada). In 1990 when the company was reorganised and became Burmah Castrol he lost Canada, but kept South America and acquired responsibility for Southern Africa, Australia and New Zealand.

Rosie Harris has had an impressive career. She is a clever, quick thinking person, and a very good strategic thinker. Her ability to plan her career, win sponsors and make friends everywhere has helped her to get to a very senior job at an unusually young age. She graduated from Birmingham University with a degree in archaeology in 1979. She was offered a place to do a PhD, but realised that she wasn't cut out to be an academic. The career counsellors at university steered her towards accountancy (a respectable career for girls).

Rosie joined Deloittes Bristol as an accountant and found that she liked it! She began to do her accountancy exams, but in 1981 had what turned out to be a good career break. She went to work for Deloittes in Bahrain. She hated it there, being the general dogsbody, but the experience was good for her. She was thrown into all sorts of situations with all sorts of clients, and learnt quickly how to be self-reliant. Her biggest achievement there was to persuade the Emir of Bahrain to pay his telephone bill!

Rosie moved to the London office of Deloittes when she qualified as a chartered accountant in 1983. She found them a good firm to work for. They encouraged her to take initiatives and to say what she thought. They were friendly and didn't slap her down for mistakes. In 1985 Rosie joined the Prudential, and in that year, after four years of marriage, Rosie and her husband began to live together in the same house full time for the first time. Previously, geographic locations had kept them apart.

Rosie found the Prudential very different from Deloittes, and for the first three months thought it was deadly. She regressed two years in responsibility. The company was bureaucratic and vast. It was a family, nannying culture. When people bought you drinks they said you've got to thank Aunty Pru for this! It was easy-going and caring, without very much pressure.

After being there a while Rosie worked out what she wanted for her career, and told her department manager (three layers above her) that she wanted his job. Three months later she got it. Rosie then began to build up her contacts around the company. Through a combination of high performance, clear career goals and a good network, Rosie climbed up the ladder to become the youngest woman to make it to middle management grade. She got a number of tough, trouble-shooting jobs which she made a success of, until in 1989, at the age of 31, she became the youngest ever financial controller of the company. Rosie's latest role is as business operations manager, reporting to the sales director.

Jim Davies is our man from Saatchi and Saatchi. He is friendly, sympathetic and quick thinking but laid-back; just what is needed in an advertising agency that specialises in good relationships with its clients. Jim got a degree from Sheffield University and started his career in 1970 with Ovaltine as an assistant product manager. He moved around in the early 1970s, taking jobs as product manager in several companies in the food and holiday industries. Then, while he was an account director with Dorland Advertising, he impressed the marketing director of Schweppes who wanted Jim working on his main products – at Saatchis. So in 1977 he joined Saatchis to work on the Schweppes account.

In 1980 Jim negotiated a year off with Saatchis, and he ended up in Australia and loved it there, but he kept running out of money so took a job with a local advertising agency to earn his return fare to London. He had a high profile there as their boy from Saatchis and won them a big account with Avis. As a result of running into his Schweppes contact at a dinner party, Jim found himself starting up an agency for Saatchis in Sydney. Jim had a good four years successfully building this agency and became its managing director. In 1988 he was invited back to Saatchis in London by his Australian friend, Bill Muirhead, the chairman of the London office, so Jim came back to London as deputy chairman. After a restructuring at Saatchis in 1990 he became a chief operating officer, running a quarter of the agency's billing.

John Nicholas, currently deputy general at the Institute of Directors, considers himself one of the early meritocrats. After being groomed by national service in the Royal Navy, he joined H and G Simonds, the brewers, in 1960. It was taken over by Courage soon afterwards. He believes he was the first young manager at Courage to be promoted to the boardroom who did not have the stereotypical background previously required; he was a non-graduate; non-shareholder; neither a member of the brewing family, nor married into it; nor was he an old Etonian or Guardsman.

John at 31 must then have been one of the youngest of his time to become a director. Like many of his aspirant and ambitious peers he readily admits fighting 'tooth and nail' to outshine colleagues and contemporaries, while at the same time 'earning his ticket' on the way up by becoming a chartered secretary, a professional qualification he regards to this day as the best all-round business qualification there is. At the same time he acquired a broad practical knowledge of the brewing industry and many of its markets and showed real achievement in the job.

Without a background that might have given his predecessors easier access to the network, he made his mark by doing whatever his boss (later to be the group managing director) asked him, and doing it just that bit better than anyone else. By performing above the norm, and by being able to adapt to the rapid changes in the company culture of the time, as it moved away from its traditional army model style of management, he managed to stand out. John did not lose heart because he was an outsider at the start. Instead, he found a way of being an indispensable insider by becoming extremely useful and by learning early on that 'knowledge is power'.

In the mid 1970s John was headhunted by Condé Nast and National Magazine Distributors Ltd, as its executive director. The first eighteen months were sheer hell. Then approaching 40, he had to learn a completely new industry and forge an entirely new career. Eventually, the publishing knowledge came. When the company lost one of its biggest clients, and other top management was replaced, John found that his face would not fit in with the new chief executive. He could not himself aspire to that job at such an early stage in the magazine industry, so he left.

He then worked for a while as an international publishing consultant, specialising in circulation and subscriptions and soon joined the board of two or three small publishing companies and on the way helped launch *BBC Wildlife* magazine. During this period he learnt the rest of the publishing game more completely while he steadily built up his contacts, and acquired more directorships. When the job as managing director of Directors Publications, the magazine publishing wing of the Institute of Directors, came up, John realised that he could combine his previous business experience with his new-found magazine publishing experience.

John did what has since been recognised as a professional publishing job, of lifting *The Director*, and in the process building up one of the most competent business teams in the game. In 1985 he was invited by the then director general, Sir John Hoskyns, to become deputy director general, and so eventually extended his publishing responsibilities to encompass all the commercial and professional activities of the IOD, the role he fulfils today.

Rosie Faunch is the general manager of the Ealing Hospital in the National Health Service. She is in charge of a general hospital and a maternity unit, where she has a budget of £25 million, and manages twelve-hundred full-time staff, including fifty-two consultants. Rosie is a lively, pretty woman, who is full of ideas and enthusiasm. She is at ease with her power and responsibilities, and combines a direct manner with a lot of charm.

Rosie started her career as a pharmacist. She left Manchester University in 1975 with a degree in pharmacy, then did a post-graduate year at the Middlesex Hospital. She worked in various hospitals as a pharmacist, and enjoyed the opportunity to work with doctors in the treatment of patients. This helped her to understand how doctors work, how they treat patients, how they make decisions, how a medical team functions and how tired a doctor can be after a night on call. At one point, when she was at Ealing Hospital, her boss went sick for eight weeks and Rosie assumed responsibility for running the pharmacy department. She was confronted with decisions and requests and had never had any training in management. She learnt more in this eight weeks than she could have learnt on a million management courses!

In 1983 Rosie was promoted to the senior pharmacist post in the district of Brent. This was the potential top of a pharmacist's career, which was usually attained by people aged up to 50; Rosie was 28! Rosie's career didn't stop there. The introduction of general management into the NHS gave her the opportunity to further her career dramatically. She took a Diploma in Management Studies and then became the unit general manager of community services in the South Bedfordshire Health Authority. Here she was in charge of district nurses, health visitors, maternity and mental handicap services. In this job she learnt about reorganising management structures and clarifying accountabilities. After nearly two years Rosie felt she had cut her teeth on general management and was ready to do something bigger, so she moved to Ealing to take up her present job as acute unit general manager.

Tom Nell comes from South Africa, but has been working for Whitbread in the UK since 1973. He is a quiet, thoughtful person with a strong sense of integrity. Tom did a BCom and LLB at Cape Town University, then joined an Anglo-American corporation mining finance company as a management trainee. He came to England in 1973 and joined Whitbread on the finance side. Starting in finance helped Tom to understand how the company fitted together and understand its key levers. But he really wanted to move into an operating job. He got a job in distribution in 1977, an area of the company which was growing in influence. This gave him his chance to move into operations through a project which involved him in working with operations people in a trading company covering the southern half of the UK. They found Tom useful and recruited him.

He spent eight years on the south coast doing a number of tough tasks – rationalising, introducing new technology and the fully harmonised hours commitment scheme. But in spite of the turmoil, his efforts to give people a sense of belonging and having fun at work created stability throughout that period. In 1986 he was asked to head up the distribution function at head office in a staff role. He helped the division to restructure nationally and to move the functions beyond cost control (Whitbread distribution now leads the brewing industry), towards an ever-increasing focus in giving customers the service they want.

In late 1988 Tom was seconded to European Cellars Ltd, a wine company. As suppliers services director he masterminded a complete restructuring of the shipping production and distribution side of the business, involving the closure of eight depots, three bonds and one production site. However, after another reorganisation he was asked back to a more mainstream job. As facilities planning manager for Whitbread Beer Company, he works on strategy for production and distribution, which he finds an interesting job.

John Mills is the director of personnel and administration for the charity Guide Dogs for the Blind, a post which he took in 1989, after a career in personnel and training in a variety of organisations. He is a down-to-earth, open person, who is not afraid to stand up for what he thinks is right.

After Cambridge University John joined Rolls-Royce in 1963 as a trainee systems analyst, but let it be known that he was interested in personnel and training. Six months later he was transferred to select and organise apprentices for external training in the apprentices training school. Then he became the factory training officer.

In 1967 he spent two years with the Road Transport Industry Training Board, where he had to deal with some aggression from member companies over the training levy. He then went to work for Fisons, the chemical company, on Humberbank. His role was to organise training and he spent a lot of time in negotiations, both with the unions and the Chemical Industry Training Board. His job moved more and more into personnel, and when he went to work for the pharmaceutical division in 1972, it was as personnel manager of a research and development unit. He became the function head of administration but parted amicably from Fisons during a reorganisation. John had a spell in a recruiting organisation but decided 'it wasn't really my bag', so joined Guide Dogs for the Blind in 1989.

CHAPTER · 2

WHAT IS POWER?

POWER ISN'T A DIRTY WORD

A manager cannot manage effectively without using power. Managerial authority and organisational politics are not black arts, they are an essential part of the process of management. Power is a positive force, giving you freedom, choice and strength, although it does carry responsibilities. Yet people are wary about power. Many managers see it as a necessary evil, or as a distasteful activity, to be shunned by people of integrity. There are those who think that organisational politics and the use of power are to be avoided if possible, and are the monopoly of self-seeking people without principle. There are certainly people like that about, but they are not in the majority. To shun politics and power is a naïve mistake, one that will put you at the mercy of powerful and influential people, and one that will bar you from many desirable and senior jobs.

Why is power such an important part of management? Why is it necessary to become involved in company politics? The reality of business life is that it is about difference; different values, different goals and different interests. There is no one clear goal or mission in a company. As a consultant I often have to ask managers to tell me about their organisation's goals. Normally I get a different answer from each manager, and often those differences are profound. I asked this question of three directors of a company producing sophisticated drugs for the medical industry. One director said that the overriding goal was to make a profit (a goal which had evaded them since they began operating eight years previously). Another director felt that scientific excellence was their main goal. A third said that the company's main aim was to survive. Behind these differing statements were a variety of different values and interests. The director who wanted to start making profits clashed with the second director who was mainly interested in the quality of scientific work. On the one hand there was a desire to free the company from dependency on government funding and the control that implied, and to achieve standing in the business world. The conflicting desire was to improve standing in the scientific world through good research and the production of innovative and life-saving drugs. The third director, who was focused on the need to survive, clashed with the second because his cost-cutting proposals threatened the research programme. But all had the company's interests at heart. All three were men of high integrity and principle. Each saw their actions as necessary for the future of the company and the actions of the others as threatening that future.

In more or less dramatic ways these differences are experienced at all levels in organisations. You may be absolutely right in your proposals, but still lose out because you aren't powerful and influential enough. Decisions in organisations are not based on logic alone, they are also determined by power and influence. If you think you have something to offer, and want to contribute towards a healthy future for your company, then you need to learn how to acquire power and influence and how to use it. To ignore it is to say – I'm not going to bother to contribute, I'm going to switch off and let the others get on with it. For managers to take this point of view is to evade responsibility, to condemn themselves to being less effective than they could, and should, be.

So, why is the wielding of power and influence seen as the darker side of managerial activity? For several reasons. There certainly are some people who pursue self-interested goals, regardless of the good of the organisation as a whole, often through foul means rather than fair. It is not surprising that people lower down in these organisations, who watch these activities from afar, are put off. It is also not surprising that they come to believe that instrumental, competitive and manipulative behaviour is inevitable, and indeed essential, for winning and moving upwards. This sort of behaviour is seen as distasteful by many, and they often choose not to get involved. They make this choice either because they haven't got the skills or the stomach for the fight, or because they aren't prepared to sacrifice their integrity.

With some people, a strong focus on the task they are performing at work diverts them from the pursuit of influence and power. For such people, an active interest in being creative or achieving goals (or both) turns them away from political activity. To be part of a team, working together to achieve group goals, openly discussing differences and measuring success by results is very rewarding for those involved. Many people in these situations just want to get on with the job rather than worry about organisational politics. Yet people who take this point of view are usually naïve when it comes to dealing with the power brokers. They may succeed when the firm is prospering, but in times of difficulty or change they lack the skills to defend those tasks and groups to which they are wedded.

There is another reason why power is seen as a dirty word. It is the view, held by many, that organisations are rational, and that decision-making is based on rationality and logic. If only, they say, we can improve the information system, perfect the organisational structure and get rid of the wheeler dealers, we could allow the organisation to perform as it should. These people think that those who engage in organisational politics are irrelevant time-wasters who only do harm.

But the reality is that power and influence are *not* evil. All managers need to be politicians if they wish to be effective, to contribute and to get on. You need to be a politician in the sense that you need to understand and be sensitive to the causes of conflict and the strategies needed to cope with conflict. You need to learn that conflict, and differences of goals, values and interests are all part of organisation life, and an inevitable part at that. There is no point in complaining about the differences and the conflict; you might as well accept that they are here to stay and learn how to deal with them. Whether you use your political skills and knowledge to promote organisational goals or to further your own aims to the detriment of the organisation is a question for your own principles and priorities. It *is* possible to be powerful and influential without being self-seeking and machiavellian. The pursuit of power is not just about building empires and putting others down. There are powerful and influential people who have the good of their company, and of their colleagues, at heart. Politics *does* have a positive side, which is about working collaboratively with other people, paying attention to their concerns and building long-term alliances.

DIFFERENT VIEWS ON POWER

The managers interviewed for this book are all people of integrity who have managed to achieve success for themselves, as well as for their departments or organisations. They have all had to involve themselves in using influence, power and company politics. Yet, even among these relatively powerful people, there is a range of views about power. Some do still find it distasteful, even though they use it.

Tom Nell from Whitbread had this to say: 'I am not a great power broker, in fact I don't want to be seen as exercising power. I think that what this business wants from you is good management, not just power.' Yet Tom recognises that he does use power to make himself a good manager, although he feels that he uses his power positively, 'not to flatten what's in front of you'.

There is a mistaken view that the only managers who are successful at scrambling to the top are those who have a lust for power and a natural talent and enthusiasm for organisational politics. So often I hear young managers say, 'I'll never make it in competition with those sorts of people, I'm just not a political animal'. Quite a few of the managers I interviewed did not have a natural inclination towards playing politics, yet they found that they had to learn how to be political, and that they were able to do so. Some learnt how to use power early on in their careers, and some didn't learn until they reached more senior positions.

Keith Manning from Bull says that he prefers to manage by consensus rather than by using power. 'Yet more recently, since I've become a member of the management committee, I've found myself using my power. It is unnatural behaviour for me, but I need to do it.'

Some managers really do dislike power politics very much indeed. They have a disregard for overt displays of power and find it distasteful. They also don't like to see people trying to influence others by creeping. Tony Hughes from Whitbread, for example, finds some politics distasteful. 'You've got to ignore negative politics and rise above it. If you are sincere and passionate you drive straight through it. But if you believe in a thing, you take actions that help you to win. So you get involved in politics to achieve goals, not for personal gain.' Tony is a very principled person, with strong beliefs and values, yet he is able to be political without losing his integrity.

Other managers have a much more favourable view of power. 'I see power as something positive,' says Mike Dearden of Burmah Castrol. 'It is the freedom to influence your environment. It comes hand-in-glove with responsibility, but I can accept that. It has improved my enjoyment of life to have more line jobs where I have more power and am more in control of my destiny than in staff jobs. I much prefer taking decisions to influencing others to take them.' People like Mike Dearden help us to see that power has a positive side; it's not just something to be used to achieve certain ends, but can bring considerable benefits.

It's not just men who enjoy being powerful, some women find it very attractive too. 'Power is feeling confident just to go out and do things, and knowing that you can do that without being slapped down,' says Rosie Harris from the Prudential. 'When you see good results, and know *you* made that decision, it makes you feel more powerful. The power to help drive the business is good. I like being powerful. I like to be in at the top. I couldn't imagine being in an organisation where I wasn't at the decision-making level.'

It's difficult to imagine what being powerful is like when you're not. Often young people at the bottom of the hierarchy only see the negative aspects; the pressures, the responsibilities, the power struggles. It is not surprising that they think it must be a different breed of human being who aspires to power. Yet power brings the freedom to do things and to make your own decisions. It can be a very heady, exciting experience to be powerful and many people find, to their surprise, that they enjoy it, in spite of the pressures.

Gaining power is also about survival, the fight to be yourself and to have some independence in a competitive world. In some organisations managers have to learn about it very quickly, especially if those organisations are very hierarchical and have strong power cultures. John Nicholas from the Institute of Directors says, 'I got line experience early and learnt about power and authority quickly. If you don't learn about power you are dependent on other people who do know how to use it.'

This book is all about getting things done in organisations as they are, not as they should be. To do that you've got to learn how to be powerful. This is not a substitute for being competent at your job, but it is an important complement.

DIFFERENT FORMS OF POWER AND HOW TO USE THEM

Power comes from many different sources. If you don't feel comfortable with one form of power, then look around for another form that fits in more easily with your values and circumstances. Tom Nell, for example, who is turned off by 'the sort of power that flattens what's in front of you', chooses instead the power of the vision, the argument and referred power. Have a look at the varied sources of power and see which you can tap into. Even if you are very junior you will find that there are some sources of power available to you. Once you start to use these sources effectively you may find that you do not remain junior for very long.

What I mean by the use of the term 'power' is the ability to get things to happen for you, and to get others to behave in certain ways or to carry out certain actions. 'Power' says Keith Manning, 'is what you take if you decide to do things. If you ask for it you won't get it.' The Latin word for power is *posse*, which means 'to be able'. Power is about using strength to control or accomplish some deed. Powerless people are weak or impotent in those situations in which they have no power. To be weak and impotent because you're powerless is a frustrating and unrewarding state in which to find yourself. It is far more healthy, both for you and for your projects, to find sources of power that you can use. What follows is a variety of different forms of power which can be acquired through your position in the hierarchy, or through your skill, your expertise or your contacts.

Position power

The most obvious source of power is the use of your position or responsibilities to get people to accept your influence and do what you want them to do. Powerful people in senior positions make sure that they keep an eye on everything that's happening within their span of control. They don't let fringe activities occur without their involvement. When you have a position of responsibility, it is important that you are seen to use the power and authority that go with that role. Some people may resist you, but most will be expecting you to use your authority and will be confused if you don't. People expect the boss to be the boss.

However, the degree of position power has changed over the years. Both Martin Smith and John Nicholas began their careers in the brewing industry in the 1960s. 'We just used our rank to get our own way, instead of using persuasion,' says Martin Smith. 'The management style was feudal,' says John Nicholas, 'authority was based on the army model. In fact, many members of the management team were from the same regiment. The managing director was the colonel and his chauffeur was his batman. The hierarchical system was straightforward. You did what you were told, you learnt the rules and kept to them.'

You can no longer use your position to give you absolute power. 'Now it's about motivation, persuasion and leading by example rather than "do as I say",' says John Nicholas. Martin Smith says, 'Now I am in the financial sector where people are very intellectual, have big egos and strong career aspirations. If you try to organise them through hierarchical power alone they will just leave.'

People expect you to use position power, but not as a substitute for all other forms of power. They accept that people in senior positions make the final decision, and carry the can. But they also expect to be consulted and informed.

Power gained from control over resources

If you have control over major investments, over hiring and firing, over what people earn and who is put where, then you will be seen as a very powerful person in your organisation. People to whom power is important seek to control both human and financial resources. Power comes from the ability to hire and fire and to change people's lives. It's quite amazing how the chairmen of major companies sometimes hang on to the decision over who gets what space in the company car park. The managing director of one company still insists on having a say in the selection of every new member of staff, down to receptionists. Although control over resources gives you power, it can cause a bottleneck if you are too insecure to delegate some of this authority. The mature manager learns how to delegate some of his or her control over resources to the right level.

Power gained from doing unpleasant things

Many managers shy away from making nasty decisions over such matters as redundancies and relocation. However, it increases other people's perception of your power if you do it yourself instead of delegating it. Of course, you've got to make it clear that you've spent time looking for other alternatives but have decided that it's the right commercial decision.

When you have to implement unpleasant decisions that you believe are commercially right, and stand by them, it tends to create a perception of power. When you have proved that there is no alternative and you implement the decision in a way that tries to retain people's self-respect and dignity – then you have a chance of earning respect. And respect tends to increase your power.

John Nicholas says, 'Not everyone can use power to make unpopular, but necessary changes. When I have to do this I try to spend time explaining the reasons to as many people as possible. Even if the initial reaction is to loathe you as an individual, most of them eventually see that the decision was right.'

Power gained from owning up to mistakes

Leaders must put themselves on the line and admit when they have made a mistake. There is a real distinction between people who can do that and those who can't. It isn't about ability, it's about mentality. If you can admit to being wrong, you signal to the world that you are strong and powerful and don't have to pretend to be infallible. If you can own up to mistakes then you needn't fear making them so much, and you can then take more risks. People who always play it safe achieve less, because they can't take risks so easily. Greg Dyke feels, 'It's best not to imagine failure and don't worry about it. If you can be like that you'll bring people around you who are similar, people who are relaxed about their careers, having fun and making achievements.'

For those people who aren't yet very senior and who haven't got access to much hierarchical power, there is still power to be gained from other sources.

Expert power

This type of power is gained by having some special skill. Financial people, computer specialists and lawyers can use skills which other people don't have, and can use these skills to influence them. John Nicholas admits to using expert power as a significant lever in his career. Early on in his working life he found himself competing with other management trainees in the brewery and at head office in London. These people were extremely competitive and John had to exert every sinew to outshine them. He did this by qualifying as a company secretary and by developing a sound, practical knowledge of the brewing marketplace. The combination of these two types of expertise made him very useful to the company when it entered its acquisition phase in the late 1960s.

Information power

This type of power comes as a result of having knowledge or information which is of use to other people. If you are up to date on the latest developments in your field, for example, this knowledge will make you powerful in your contact with people who need it, but haven't got it. This type of power is closely allied to expert power. John Nicholas provides an example of how knowledge and information confers power. 'Knowledge is power. I have always had a good retentive memory. When people had problems to solve they would often rely on me, either because I had the information, or knew where to get it. The sort of information required has to be practical, useful knowledge of what is needed for success in your industry. I was increasingly invited to join working parties and attend problem-solving meetings. I became not just a useful, but eventually an essential, contributor to those meetings.' A fertile brain and sound knowledge can be a formidable combination.

There are lots of people in what could be described as back-room jobs who have information power, but who don't know how to use it. People in personnel, technical or legal departments can use their specialist knowledge to make themselves useful and get noticed. Accountants have strong possibilities here. Rosie Harris, for example, finds that she has information power. 'People in the company come to me for information. Having information makes you very powerful. I've got to know what's going on. I'm always looking for the story behind the numbers.'

Another aspect of information power is the power you get from knowing how the system works. This can be very important in a big company. John Nicholas learnt all about the arterial systems when working at head office. Later, when he became the free trade director of the eastern region, this knowledge enhanced his power to get things done quickly and effectively.

Power of the vision

If you are the sort of person who has good ideas, and who is prepared to commit yourself to them and fight for them enthusiastically, you will find this an important source of power. Not everyone has good ideas and people will look up to those who do. Greg Dyke reached the position he is at now in the television world by having ideas and by using his tremendous energy to convince others about them.

Tony Hughes of Whitbread is another manager who gains in power through being a visionary. 'Once I am convinced about a cause I get very committed and fight for it passionately. However, watch you don't go fighting lost causes, it's dangerous!' People are impressed by someone who has a clear vision of the future, who knows what they want and has worked out how to get there. The energy that goes along with having a vision and being committed to an idea is attractive and powerful. High-energy people tend to be more powerful and appealing than low-energy people. Tony has gained a lot of personal power through his energy and alertness.

Referent power

This type of power comes when people want to identify with you, or be with you or like you. Successful people often find that others in their field want to be associated with them or use them as role models. Jim Davies from Saatchis recognises that he has a degree of referent power. 'There is a very clear culture in Saatchis. All the bright young managers know who's in and who's out. They see that it's good to be with Jim because he is close to the managing director.'

The other side of the coin to referent power is *referred* power. This is the power you get from being associated with someone powerful. For example, you will enjoy referred power if you are close to the managing director. This also gives you referent power, since people will see you as someone good to be associated with. And your subordinates will in turn enjoy referred power from this association. Of course, you can take this too far. People who constantly involve themselves in name dropping are seen as creeps who are so insecure that they need props in the form of famous friends.

However, referred power can be used constructively. If you happen to know that someone very senior is in favour of something you're trying to get to happen, then it can strengthen your case to make this clear. Then you are tapping into the referred power of that senior person. But you will need to get out and about to find out what views senior people hold, if you want to use referred power in this way. You can actually use referred power by bluffing if you're desperate, but it only works for a while until you get found out.

Do watch out for the 'flavour of the month' aspect. If you ally yourself to someone who is only temporarily 'in', your referent power will be short lived and you too may tumble from favour along with your god.

The power of the argument

You can derive a certain amount of power from being articulate, and from being able to argue your case coherently and persuasively. If you are hesitant and poor with words, it does detract from your personal power and influence, even though your ideas may be sound. Managers who take the time and trouble to explain things to the workforce, and who put their case well, increase their power by doing so. Tom Nell from Whitbread feels that he has increased his power by 'making complex issues accessible to folk in language they can understand'.

> In the early 1980s when I had an operating role I decided to explain to the workforce just how the business operated and year-end profits. I took people in chunks and explained it to them in terms they understood. As a result of this effort I had the largest number of applicants for the company's save-as-you-earn scheme. It also made it easier for me to negotiate. I introduced a new salary scheme which took six months to negotiate. The workforce accepted it because I managed to explain flexibility to them, for example, in terms that stopped it being a hated concept. Once they understood how the company was going to use (not abuse) flexibility, the strong initial resistance was overcome. The scheme is still operating and both management and workforce have won together.

When people are in conflict, those who can stay calm, collect their thoughts and express their point of view have the most power. The person who gets overexcited and loses the ability to speak coherently also loses some power.

Power from image and trappings

Many people seek to increase their power and status by surrounding themselves with trappings such as expensive desks, flashy cars, smart briefcases etc. This will only work if you also have genuine power from other sources. Often managers try to enhance their power by getting their secretaries to limit access to them. If people find it difficult to get through to you because you're busy and important then this does denote some status, but it can also have a negative effect on your power. If you shut yourself away surrounded by the trappings of power – with a dragon-like secretary – you can't actually exercise the power you think you have. If you want to be powerful you've got to be on the court where the ball is moving about. You've got to be involved and accessible, see and be seen, keep your door open and reply to letters.

The power of values

Having strong and consistent values can give you power. 'Believing in things and sticking by your beliefs does give you power,' says Tony Hughes. 'I really don't like it when managers say, "these are my values and beliefs and if you don't like them I'll change them." My core values are sacrosanct to me. I won't compromise. If the company's values aren't the same, then mine will prevail.' People who pay lip-service and who jump on the bandwagon are seen as followers rather than leaders. Tony is so convinced of his values about management and organisations that he has been very successful at Whitbread in convincing people to go along with his projects.

PERSONAL POWER VS ORGANISATIONAL POWER

Some sources of power are organisational, such as position power and control over resources. Other sources of power are personal, such as the power of values and the power of the argument. Personal power comes from the way you behave, rather than from your position. If you combine your organisation power (however small that may be) with personal power, then this makes you much more influential. The nice thing about power is that because it has so many different sources, everybody can have *some* power and influence if they become aware of the sources available to them. Becoming powerful is partly a matter of spotting opportunities, waking up to the power you already have and letting it strengthen you, and developing strategies for increasing your power. The next four chapters will demonstrate how you can do this.

Negative personal power

Power is a strong and constructive force in management, because it gains you respect and enables you to get things done. However, all forms of power can be used either positively to reward or negatively to harm. Negative power is exercised by people who are compensating for their psychological problems. These people feel vulnerable for some reason, and manipulate and take power away from others in order to protect themselves. They can be overbearing, dominating and arrogant.

Although negative power may produce results in the short term, it is an unhealthy way to manage. From a personal point of view, people who use negative power to compensate for psychological problems never seem to solve their inner problems, and are often quite unhappy people. Negative power also produces problems for the people on the receiving end.

> The problem is how do you manage it? When people lurch from vitriolic to caring styles it does sap the energy of their subordinates. Some people cope with it by ignoring it and not standing up to their boss. The problem is that over the years you can become a person who accedes on *every* issue, even on the serious ones about which you should make a stand.

Managers who are too dominating attract around them people with strong dependency needs. Able people, who are personally strong, will simply leave if they are on the receiving end of too much negative power. The danger is that you get left with the weaker, more dependent people who need to be dominated. Thus, the negatively powerful leader is constantly frustrated by the weakness of his staff, but is unable to keep productive people around him.

Rosie Faunch gives an example of negative power being used by a manager in the National Health Service.

> This manager, whom I shall call Dave, had the power to make strategic and operational decisions about the health authority. He was aggressive, chauvinistic, territorial and an empire builder. He was not a leader, but a manipulator. Until a different type of person came to manage him (my boss) and I took over management of the hospital, nobody had been strong enough to manage or challenge him.
>
> When I took up my job I started to challenge his decisions, and I succeeded because I was backed by my boss. The more Dave's power base was leached, the more aggressive he became. He couldn't adapt to the changed climate in the health service, and couldn't understand that the process of general management means empowering people in the organisation to take their own decisions.
>
> Another senior manager who worked for me used her professional position to prevent her staff from developing a less hierarchical approach to their jobs. I, as her boss, was not 'allowed' to meet with her staff unless she was there or had discussed the agenda with them. I was once 'told off' for phoning one of them up! Needless to say the arrangement didn't last too long, and it was intriguing to hear what crawled out of the woodwork after she had departed. The sad thing was that her motives were good,

but she hadn't realised that you can't use personal power to halt progress for ever.

Another type of negative power comes from people who don't necessarily seek to be negatively powerful, but who are articulate, challenging and quick thinking. They make decisions quickly and can be experienced as arrogant and dismissive by lesser mortals. In the end, by being so overpowering, these managers actually diminish their own power. People are afraid to confront them, to test new ideas out with them or to give them information that they won't want to hear. No one likes to lose face or be rubbished by a brilliant but overpowering boss. So, to protect themselves, subordinates will withhold unpleasant but important information, fail to raise marginal issues and spend a lot of time working out ways to influence such a boss. All of this slows down and distorts the decision-making process and threatens the quality of decisions.

Positive personal power

Personal power comes from the way you behave, but this is strongly linked with how you feel about yourself inside. Positive personal power comes from maturity, feeling secure in your relationships, not needing to gain at the expense of others and confidence in your inclinations. You are strong because you trust yourself. Your behaviour is not overly determined by a need to conform, to be liked, to rebel, to control or manipulate others. You are relatively autonomous and decisive, and have a strong sense of responsibility. Thus personal power is an inner strength and is available to anyone, regardless of their seniority.

All the managers I interviewed for this book had personal power. They all had confidence in themselves and a personal strength derived from a trust in their own judgement. Positive personal power is attractive; it makes people feel they want to associate with you, trust you and pay attention to what you have to say. You'll find it much easier to influence people if you have personal power and are able to use it positively.

The responsibility of power

Having and using power does carry responsibilities. If you have the power to influence events and to make decisions, you need to ensure that you do this with the good of others in mind, not just for your own gain.

Power carries another responsibility which powerful people don't often think about. Not everyone has power, or feels powerful. People who see themselves as weak or powerless can feel put down and diminished by powerful people. These weaker people often see power as being in limited supply. If one person has it then the other cannot. So they feel that the stronger person's power is reducing their own. For example, people who are indecisive can feel inferior and powerless when faced with strong people who make decisions quickly, without obvious anxiety and hesitation. People finding themselves in this position may attack in subtle, indirect ways, trying to inhibit you, the stronger person, from your leadership by making you feel guilty. They may comment that they find you overpowering. They can make you feel that you are denying them something they need, or trampling over them.

Powerful people have to become sensitive to the feelings they generate in other people, and to their power needs. Although powerless people are concerned with issues of power, powerful people don't usually think about this subject at all. They are accustomed to making things happen with their power and usually just get on with it. But having power does mean having more responsibility, and you do need to combine your powerful behaviour with supportiveness, so that you are not experienced as threatening by other people. Your power is enhanced by having able people around you. So you need to use your power in a way which attracts such people, not in a way which inhibits or repels them.

PATRISM AND MATRISM

Psychologists have identified two fundamentally different approaches to power which they call 'patrism' and 'matrism'.

● *Patrism* is the traditionally male form of leadership: tough (as opposed to radical and tender) and based on a belief in order, discipline and respect for authority.[1] It values self-control and rational behaviour and makes a strong distinction between male and female behaviour. It puts faith in age and experience rather than youth. Managers wielding this form of power use people and ignore their needs. They make occasional grand gestures but don't really think about people's personal needs and problems:

> I have a client who makes 'grand gestures'. He has a subordinate who is
> under terrible pressure, so much so that he is drinking too much and
> beginning to make poor decisions at work. What this person needs is help
> in reducing the pressure and support from his boss. Instead of that, the
> boss sends him on a holiday to the Caribbean. Great, but he comes right
> back to the pressure and soon everything is as bad as it was before.[2]

The quickest way to power is the old, traditional way – ignore people's
needs and use them.

● *Matrism*, on the other hand, is a form of leadership that prefers
discussion to just giving orders. It is optimistic about the future,
believes in openness and makes little distinction between the sexes. It
relies on expertise rather than experience, and values youth and imagination rather than age.[1]

It would be a gross over-simplification to say that all powerful men use
patrism and all powerful women use matrism. Many pioneering business women in tough environments have developed extreme forms of
patrism, and see it as their only means of survival. And conversely,
although most men do still use patrism, there is a noticeable swing, in
both the UK and the US, towards matrism. There is a growing sense
among top-level managers that in order to achieve significant change
they must pay attention to the needs of their people: 'the only route to
success for leaders is to nurture and facilitate rather than to police'.

There is a price to be paid when macho, aggressive leaders favour
patrism and it is paid personally by the people using it – as well as by
their organisations. This model of leadership and power is to show
outward strengths, to cover up weaknesses and to hide inner anxieties.
You don't own up when you don't know; you pretend you *do* know and
bluff your way through. You stay tough and don't talk about how it feels.
This leads to a feeling of isolation because you can't share your feelings,
so you think that it's just you suffering from anxiety, insecurity and
inner conflicts. The myth is that, in order to get on, you must compete
with everyone.

Patrism, with its belief in order and discipline, is a form of leadership
and power that does not cope easily with change and uncertainty. These
leaders, when faced with uncertainty, polarise problems into black or
white, react negatively rather than take the initiative, flare up, withdraw,
work harder and longer, and escape into drinking bouts or other forms

of harmful behaviour. Eventually they may break down. This is hardly a healthy model for a manager to imitate.[2]

Matrism is a form of power which can give you a successful style of leadership. It enables you to combine positive personal power with caring about others, and with being non-threatening to most people. There will be insecure or vulnerable people who see your power as a threat, however positive and supportive you try to be. They will use negative power strategies against you, undermine your leadership and endanger your position if they can. You need to be alert to these dangers and have your own power defence strategies ready for such encounters. Chapter 13 is about defending yourself from dirty politics.

Power is a state of mind, as well as a result of position, policies and practices. It's far too easy to say, 'I can't get things to happen because of all of the other buggers around me, it's their fault.' You will always have some power if you seek it. If you believe in what you're doing there will be opportunities to influence events, but you've got to seek those opportunities, and practise being powerful. Keith Manning has learnt to be more powerful than he used to be. Now he goes to the board and says, 'Here is my solution, here are my arguments, and I'm going to implement them unless you have any objections.' It doesn't always work, but as an approach it stands a better chance than, 'Here is my case, will you give me permission to implement?' If you can't achieve objectives by the direct use of power, then seek another route, through influencing the people who do have power. Don't abuse your power, but develop it and use it – otherwise it'll be someone else making the decisions, and they may not be right.

WHAT IS INFLUENCE?

POWER AND INFLUENCE

Why have a chapter on influence, you may ask. Isn't it enough to be powerful, and anyway, aren't power and influence the same thing? The two words *are* often used together, but they don't have the same meaning. Power is a resource – it's the ability to get things to happen to you. Influence is what you achieve by using your power. It's about getting things done through other people. Influence implies the capability to change other people's behaviour patterns and the decisions they take, or otherwise to affect events without actually having the power to do so. It's the art of getting the donkey to run or stop without using the stick.[3]

The managers I spoke to saw a very clear distinction in practice between influence and power. 'Influence is different from power,' says Roger French. 'To achieve power you've got to have won battles. This is not so with influence – it's more about behaviour and attitudes.'

How to use influence

'Power is the ability to take decisions yourself, whereas influence is the ability to affect the decisions of others.' Mike Dearden is an example of someone who enjoys using power, and who feels strengthened by it. He therefore sees influence in a rather negative light. 'There are more negative connotations about influence – although it doesn't need to be negative, you can steer towards a worthy decision. Influence has a covert feeling. Power is more open; with it you have more responsibility. Influence has less responsibility attached to it.' Other mangers, with less of a taste for power, see influence as the preferred route to getting things done.

People working in head offices or in staff, rather than line management jobs, can normally only resort to influence, because their position power is limited. Managers in line jobs do have more power to make their own decisions and tell people what to do. But even *they* must learn to be influential in order to deal with bosses and managers of other departments – people over whom they have no direct power. It's amazing how even quite junior people in other departments can block you if you've failed to influence them. It's very important to develop your ability to influence, because no one ever has unlimited power, even over their subordinates.

As a young management consultant, the most helpful thing I did was to establish a firm friendship with the two printers who produced our reports and proposals. I could always get a document printed on time, even if I drafted it a day before the deadline. My friends in the print shop would simply allow me to jump the queue. I can remember my boss being enraged when an important report of his had been delayed because the print shop was working on one of mine. His mistake was to blow up at me, instead of building a relationship with the printers himself and thus negotiating a better place in the queue. Theoretically, he had the power to tell the printers to put my work aside, but he couldn't use his power because he had no influence over them.

So how do we make ourselves influential? It's a combination of:

- knowing who to influence and how to go about it;
- being skilful in your behaviour so that people want to pay attention to you and to co-operate with you.

Don't rely on formal channels

As with power it is common for politically naïve managers to assume that the only way to influence decisions is through formal channels. Although formal channels should be used, if you rely on them entirely you will find that you have lost out to people who know how to use the informal network. The first step in becoming an influential manager is to learn how the informal system works, and to try to become part of it. Make sure you're not on the outside of the informal network. If you are, you'll either be ignored or you'll become the butt of people's jokes, and suffer at the hands of more political people.

It does take time to learn the informal system, but all the managers I interviewed found that it was essential. Tom Nell says:

It took me a long time to find out how it all operated. I initially misunderstood the process at work. I thought you could influence simply by using argument and logic. I thought that if I got my thinking straight the task was done. My law background inclined me to think that way. I started learning about influencing when I had my first operating role. In order to make things happen and to change things I began to look for more effective routes. When I was trying to make changes I found myself up against a lot of inertia. People were not sure how the change would affect them, and not sure if they trusted management. These situations were just not susceptible to straight logic, above and below.

GETTING INTO INFORMAL NETWORKS

Whether you like it or not, informal networks are already well established in most organisations. If you don't get included in these informal groups your isolation will limit your influence. In these networks people exchange information about who has the power, about acceptable ways of behaving, about the culture of the company, about influence strategies and about how to pull strings. You also learn how to avoid doing things that might make you lose friends and influence. Thus, through these networks you gain access to information, powerful allies and the social contacts you need for support. You'll discover who to approach before a meeting in order to get support for your views, for example. Contacts can also help protect you when you're on the receiving end of unfair treatment or power plays.

There is no automatic entry to these networks. You have to appreciate their value and make an effort to fit in and join. Quite often women, or technical and 'back-room' people tend to be excluded, either because they perceive networking as a political and time-wasting activity, or because they simply get on with their work and don't give networking a thought.

If you are excluded you do pay a price. You don't learn to see the political environment accurately – you simply don't have access to the information that would explain it to you. You probably won't grasp the importance of the political system as a legitimate way of getting things done, and will become baffled and frustrated by your inability to gain recognition and influence. People finding themselves in this position can become bitter about their lack of power and influence, and will be turned off by the activities of more politically aware managers. This reinforces their isolation, as bitter cynical people will be avoided by their colleagues, particularly by those with a more positive point of view who are learning to get things done by working the system.

When you join an organisation the informal network can help enormously with your apprenticeship – if you take the trouble to make friends as well as learn the job. Through the network you will get to know people who can assist you in learning about the company's beliefs and attitudes and discover appropriate methods for getting things done. If you lack access to these networks your apprenticeship will be slower, more painful and less complete. As a result you may develop values and attitudes that are markedly different from those of your colleagues, thus reinforcing your difficulties in fitting in and influencing.

What can you do to overcome these barriers? The first step is to recognise informal networking as a legitimate way of getting things done. Competence without the ability to make things happen means wasting a lot of effort. If no one outside your office or section knows about you, then you are of limited value to the organisation. To be able to contribute fully you need to be in touch with what's going on and who is doing it.

How to build a network

There is nothing mysterious about the art of making contacts, you just have to put yourself about, avoid getting buried in work and make friends! Make friends wherever you can, and not just in your own office or department. Avoid specialising in your own job to the extent that you don't get to learn about the rest of your organisation. Getting to know your company's business doesn't just help you to understand better how your section fits in, it is also a way of making contacts across the organisation. When you move to a new job find out who does what, pick up the phone or drop into your new colleagues' offices and arrange to meet them informally to find out about their side of things. Some people may be too busy to see you, but most will appreciate your interest. The politically astute will understand what you're trying to do and will help you with your contact building.

Roger French puts a lot of effort into building and maintaining his network of contacts in Coopers Deloitte.

Even though I'm on the consulting side I've kept in touch with the auditing and tax sections. I meet people by attending company events – social events, training courses and market product launches. I also get involved in interdepartmental projects. All of this gives you a broader perspective, which helps to make you more influential anyway, apart from the advantage of providing you with good contacts.

Martin Smith found when he moved into the US banking sector that he had to rely on being influential through building up a network of contacts and sponsors.

In this you have to rely on influence. Citibank was as political as any organisation anywhere, because they overhire – both in terms of numbers and quality of staff. The place was stuffed with able, aggressive, tough people with very ambiguous definitions of their responsibilities. It was a matrix management system. I was responsible for London, but the chiefs in New York were responsible for the functions. So my staff reported both to me and to their New York bosses. I had to build up my influence through a system of sponsorship. I made sure that I got to know the people in New York. I found that much of my power and influence derived from my contacts in New York, rather than merit.

Rosie Harris really got started on building her networks when she attended a development course for aspiring women managers at the Prudential. 'The course helped me to understand other areas of the company. I had made some contacts before the course through being an auditor, but I didn't know any senior women. They proved to be very good contacts. With every new job I did in the Pru I met people in other parts of the company. I volunteered to present to senior people as a way of increasing my visibility, even though I hate presenting.' Networking can be so much harder for women, yet Rosie found a way round these problems. She used the contacts she made on the women's course very well. If there are other women managers in your company, get to know them. Women are now learning the value of networking and the price of isolation, and they will often put themselves out to help other women. But women can't confine their contact building to their own sex, there just aren't enough of them! Rosie has taken the trouble to make friends with people of both sexes. She arranges lunches and drinks after work. She doesn't make the mistake of rushing off home after work every evening; she knows how important it is to spend time networking.

Don't let being a woman stop you from building a network. Attend away days, lunches for managers and mix with your colleagues and their spouses socially. Go to everything, from parties to a rugby international. It will pay off for you professionally.

Once you have begun to make friends you will start to learn from them that there is always a system that bypasses large sections of the proper channels of authority. You will learn that you must always ask of any system, 'Who is really in charge?' It is this person that you need to influence, either directly if you have his or her ear, or indirectly through people he or she trusts and will listen to. Remember, the person who has the power may or may not be the person in the title-holding role.

Sometimes, entry into the power networks can be difficult, for women, for new and junior people and for racial minorities. It may not be immediately obvious how to make friends and contacts in these networks, especially if the people you work with day to day don't belong in them. First, you have to identify the gatekeepers. Who are the people informally responsible for recruiting new members? Once you have established who these people are, try to make contact, either informally at company social events or through getting to work on projects that bring you into contact with them. Perhaps you can get to know them by asking for their advice or help on some work you are involved in. Once you've got to know some of them well enough you can ask one to act as your sponsor for entry to the desired network. It may be something that seems quite innocent, like getting to join their exclusive drinking or squash sessions. No matter, brush up on your squash strokes and join in, it may be a really positive career move.

Staying in

Getting into a network is one step, but staying in is another. If you don't fit for some reason, you won't stay. 'In-groups' are dynamic and elusive things. They move on, change venues, change fashions etc. You can find yourself left out in the cold playing squash with the other people who didn't quite make it, while the real in-crowd are now gathering at the bungie-jumping club.

To stay in the network and exert influence through it, you've got to adhere to what the network finds acceptable. If they all wear black shoes, don't turn up in brown. (Remember that white socks will get you excluded from most power networks!) On a more serious note don't challenge those values and habits which are sacred to the network. If the in-crowd are all solid, grey family men, and you try to bounce in as a debonair bachelor with a string of lovelies in your address book, you'll be seen as a challenge. If they believe in mushroom management, and you hold the view that managers should spend most of their time communicating, then you'll be ejected as a threat. If you find that the values of the desired network stick in your throat and you feel really uncomfortable about even paying lip-service to them, then you have a dilemma. It's difficult to be seen as a good person if you're being untrue to yourself and it hurts. Anyway, nobody likes creeps. People who are instrumental in their relationships are usually spotted and avoided. If you find yourself in this position it may be worth considering a change of job, and a move to an organisation where you are in harmony with the values of the power élite. It is difficult to influence people if you have no values or culture in common.

Once you're established in the network, life gets easier and you are genuinely more influential. Managers in the network make deals with each other. Individuals or groups agree to support each other to agree a common purpose, as long as there are benefits for everyone. You get to know each other's aims and can agree over how not to interfere with them. You will have access to powerful allies who will support you when you are under threat or when you need to effect a change.

Building long-term alliances

Don't make the mistake of only using the network for short-term gains. The astute manager builds up a series of long-term alliances. He or she stays in touch with people even when there are no favours to be asked. In fact, if you only bother to see people when you need something from them they will find the relationship rather unrewarding, and you may not even achieve your short-term aims. People who are treated instrumentally feel free to respond in kind. You never know when you might need help from a particular quarter, and if you can phone a friend you may have known for years it's a real boon. Many of us are disinclined to think long term.

> I think I am bad at networking. Short termists like me don't think about networking for the future. When I need to sell work this month, I don't think about phoning someone who will give me work next year.

The clever manager will have longer-term projects which he uses to keep in touch with contacts, even when he is under pressure to achieve short-term aims.

SKILLS THAT HELP US TO BE INFLUENTIAL

While the first step in becoming influential is to become politically aware, that alone isn't enough. Even if you gain access to the right people, you won't influence them unless you are skilful in your behaviour. In fact, the actions of a politically aware manager who is unskilful in his or her behaviour can be dramatically counter-productive. If you fear that you cannot even make it to square one because you are shy, socially awkward or because you have a tendency to put your foot in it, then don't lose heart. Certainly, contact building is easier for people with good social skills, but you can brush up on these skills if you need to. The rest of this chapter describes the sort of behaviour that will help you to influence, but if you feel you need more try to get your company to send you on an interpersonal skills course.

INFLUENTIAL BEHAVIOUR

Here are some tips on behaviour which will help you to be influential the next time you deliberately or accidentally run into your managing director in the corridor. Remember though, that influential behaviour is not just something you can turn on when you need it. It helps to have an influential image and this has implications for your behaviour all the time you are at work.

Influencing others is a process which can be seen in three stages.

- *Getting in* starts it all off. Here you get the other person to pay attention and give you a chance to influence them.
- *Getting action* is where you influence them to accept your suggestion or act in the way you want them to.
- *Getting out* is the art of leaving the other person genuinely influenced by you, and not inclined to change their mind or give your request low priority.

Getting in: how to start influencing a person

This first stage is vitally important to the process of influencing someone. If you cannot get that person to listen with an open mind to your proposal and at least give you a chance to influence them, then you will get nowhere. If you are trying to persuade someone who listens politely but clearly has their mind closed to your proposals right from the start, you have failed.[2]

It's very important to your eventual success to recognise that you stand no chance of influencing someone if you cannot pass this first stage. There are usually barriers and resistances to be overcome before the other person will let down their natural defences. You need to be aware that there will be issues around like this.

- Do I trust this person?
- Will I lose out if I accept this proposal?
- Will my life-style be affected?
- Do I like and respect this person enough to want to deal with them?
- Do I feel that this person is credible – have they the necessary seniority/experience/authority?
- Do they look influential?
- Do I feel comfortable with them?
- Do I have the authority to give a decision?

Let's look at these issues and see what you need to do at this initial stage to make it more likely you will succeed. Getting in means dealing with the other person's initial concerns and making a start on building a good relationship. This depends on a number of factors.

Trust The other person needs to trust you before they will do what you ask, particularly if this involves taking risks. The more trustworthy one person becomes to another, the more influence he or she will have. Your influence over someone is very much a question of how much you are trusted in the broadest sense. John Mills finds that he is given a lot of leeway within broad policy directives by the council of Guide Dogs for the Blind. His initial influence strategy had to be to build this trust, and having done so, his ability to act and influence are considerably enhanced.

You can begin to build trust at an early stage by showing interest, empathy, integrity and openness. Obviously, in the end, people will trust you if you prove yourself to be trustworthy by your actions. But in the initial stages when you haven't yet had a chance to prove yourself, trust is a major issue. If you look a person in the eye and behave as if you have nothing to hide, it is more likely that they will *want* to trust you. If you avoid eye contact people will think you are devious and untrustworthy. At this early stage, when there is nothing else to go on, other than your behaviour, they will pay a lot of attention to things like eye contact and openness when assessing whether to trust you or not.

Personal gain or loss Quite often people don't give you the chance to influence them because of concerns about things that they hesitate to talk openly about. If you don't show that you are willing to discuss *all* issues sympathetically and don't encourage them to say what's on their mind, you may fall at the first post. It's very frustrating to be resisted by a person who is not giving the real reason for his or her reluctance. You can't win arguments like these. If the other person doesn't raise the real issues you can't deal with them.

Tom Nell has had some experience with these hidden agendas:

> I sometimes get a lot of inertia from people who aren't sure how a change or proposal will affect them. They are often concerned about the effect on their standard of living, but this is never directly expressed. I have to help folk to overcome the emotives, but I don't do it by telling them not to be emotional! I look for a series of steps that help them to move from fear, suspicion and caution to feeling comfortable with the change. I have to put myself in their shoes. I feel that the class system stops many English managers from doing this. I look for statements that give comfort in the area of greatest concern. I need to express their concerns for them. That makes it easier for them to feel easy about expressing and solving the difficulty. You've got to try to understand the barriers. Avoid being blinded by your own assumptions, you've got to work out what the other person's are. I've worked a lot on non-logical barriers, and what to do to overcome them.

Anxiety Anxiety is usually present at the getting in stage, whether it's anxiety about hidden agendas or not. The main cause of anxiety is uncertainty. The other person will remain anxious until they know why you are there and what you're going to ask them to do. You will also be anxious until you have made your intentions clear. So come to the point early in your conversation, and don't keep them guessing. Find out early on what the other person is concerned about, and try to reassure them over these issues.

Rapport It is much more difficult to influence a person who doesn't like you or feel comfortable with you. Building rapport helps at the getting in stage because it helps people to feel comfortable with you and to feel relaxed about expressing their concerns. Rapport is established by being attentive to the other person, looking at them, and listening and responding to them. You need to empathise and encourage them so that they feel you are genuinely interested and concerned. Smiles and eye contact will help. If, instead, you rattle off your arguments with a scowl of concentration, this may be an understandable product of your anxiety, but it will not inspire trust and the other person will be less inclined to give you a chance to influence them. Serious, intense or cold people will often fail simply because they do not attempt to build rapport.

Keith Manning pays a lot of attention to building rapport:

> You are mistaken if you think that you can get a sale by doing everything right. You have to get close to the person and build a relationship. Then it's easier to make the sale. I think I win their respect. I persuade people to do things by becoming credible to them. I get friends and sponsors by communicating well with them and trying to understand what they're trying to achieve, what motivates them and what they want for themselves. Then I have the information to modify what I am offering to interest them. I can only do this by talking to them a lot and often.

Credibility There are two factors which determine your credibility: your behaviour, and being alert to what the other person is looking for.

Your behaviour is critical in establishing credibility. Other people will respond to you more easily if you *look* influential. Being visibly anxious yourself and making an elaborate presentation of your qualifications and expertise is likely to arouse anxiety and distrust. On the other and, if you walk, speak and sit with the quiet confidence and authority of someone who knows what they are doing then people are more likely to find you credible.

Being alert to what the other person is looking for is also important. Managing directors and production people want 'the bottom line' and want to know how you're going to achieve it, while chairmen and research and development people want a long philosophical discussion on your thinking behind the proposal. Some people want to know the upsides *and* the downsides when someone is trying to influence them.

Mike Dearden is switched on to what the other person is looking for:

My previous MD was interested in the detail. Your proposition had to stand up to an examination on detail otherwise he would not consider it. My present MD is much more interested in the thinking behind the proposal. If he likes your strategy and logic then he will talk to you about it, and he will not worry too much about the detail.

Are you influencing the right person? Sometimes you fail because the person you're trying to influence doesn't have the authority to make the decisions. Make sure you've identified the person with the power, or someone with access to the power, before you waste any time.

Getting in may take a few minutes, several hours or several meetings, but until you have achieved this, you won't be able to exert any influence. John Mills thinks that it's very important to be alert at this stage. 'You've got to sum people up quickly, and it can be difficult if you don't know them. You've got to make assumptions based on their jobs and background. You'll pick up clues but you've got to test them.' Once you begin to see that the other person is opening his or her mind to your proposals, it is time to bring your strategy for getting action into play.

Getting action

Planning ahead

If you have the opportunity, you'll increase your chances of success if you plan your approach before you speak to the person you're trying to influence. Ask yourself the following questions.

• What are the factors which could make me fail?
• What are the factors which could help me to succeed?

Then draw up a chart like the one below with the resisting forces on one side and the helping forces on the other.

Helping forces	Resisting forces

Suppose for example you are trying to persuade a line manager to adopt the company's new people management strategy. Here is what your chart might look like.

Helping forces	Resisting forces
Managing director in favour	Production director thinks it's a waste of time
Training courses in people management are available and popular	She hasn't got good people skills
Most other managers have adopted the strategy	She thinks that only operational results are worth worrying about, not people issues
She won't get her promotion if she doesn't implement the people management strategy	She hasn't got time to worry about people management

In practice, this list is likely to be a lot longer. Some of the forces will be much stronger than others and should be weighted. The next stage in your planning is to identify those forces over which you have some control, so that you take them into account when you are preparing your case. Usually, it's less pressurising to try to reduce the resisting forces than to build on the helping forces, but you can do both. In this case you could reduce her resistance by offering training in people skills and time management. You could also show how delegation and target setting can actually save time in the end by enabling her staff to achieve results with less input from her. This would be less confrontational than pointing out that the managing director is behind you and threatening her with missing a promotion. Thinking through the issues beforehand like this can make you much more on the ball when you're face-to-face with the person you're trying to persuade. Anticipating the scope and nature of any resistance will help you to plan your strategy and arguments, and give you a better chance of success.

So many people make the mistake of failing to plan properly. They think through their arguments, convince themselves and then go into battle assuming victory because of the strength of their logic. Then they are surprised and unprepared by resistance based on someone else's logic, and on the politics of the situation. Don't let this happen to you. A few minutes spent planning and talking things through with helpful colleagues can save hours of argument and frustration.

Choosing your influence strategy

There are two basic approaches.

The *push strategy* is effective when you know where you want to go or are clear about the solution to the problem. This is a directive strategy in which there are a number of stages.

1. Set the scene, identify the problem or opportunity and make your proposal for the solution.
2. Invite reactions.
3. Summarise your discussions and check that you understand each other.
4. Deal with the objections, either by persuasion or authority, depending on whether you want commitment or compliance.
5. Agree on the outcome – who is going to do what and by when.[2]

It is quite a strong, powerful approach, and the art is to avoid making the other person feel overwhelmed or rebellious. Be clear and firm about your proposals, but also be approachable so that the other person can feel free to discuss them and raise any concerns.

Here is an example of the push strategy from Tom Nell:

When I was working in European Cellars it was very much influenced by the old Grant's style, which was – things don't normally change very much. But we got into a position where we *had* to change, and we had to reduce the workforce dramatically. The board of directors had never been through that level of disruption before. My task was to persuade my board colleagues that we could manage the changes better, by announcing them early. I had to persuade them that it was in our interests to be open and clear about the need for change.

I solved the problem by explaining that we planned behind closed doors. The higher the risk, the more managers we involved in planning, the better the plans and higher the commitment to it. The directors' objections were initially strong and there was a lot of concern and I had to deal with them carefully. Finally, I helped them feel that they were in safe hands and that I and my team wouldn't let them down. I convinced them that I had had experience of redundancies before and that early announcement and sharing the problem with everyone had helped rather than hindered. I won individuals over by painting a picture of what it would be like and one by one they agreed to go along with me. Then we got down to the detailed planning.

The *pull strategy*, on the other hand, depends on arriving at a joint agreement on what to do, rather than on one person's authority. This is most effective when the other person's commitment is essential. This strategy also has several stages.

1. State your view of the problem.
2. Clarify how the other person sees the situation.
3. Work for an agreement over the existence of the problem or opportunity.
4. Look for a solution, using as many of the other person's ideas as possible, especially if their commitment is important.
5. Come to a joint agreement on what is going to be done.[2]

The pull strategy calls for quite a different set of skills from the push strategy. Here you need to let the other person know you are pulling together. You need to be supportive so that they are encouraged to make their own suggestions. Where there are differences of opinion you need to look for common ground and build on any aims or interests you share. The most powerful thing you can do is appeal to the other person's imagination. Get them to picture how things could be in the future if you are able to go forward. Once a person starts to build visions of the future, he or she is close to being committed. You can help them to visualise the future by painting pictures with words of how things could be.

This is an example of the 'pull' strategy:

I had to speak to the staff in the accounts department on the need to invoice early and chase debtors so as to keep our cash flow in a healthy state. I called a meeting and explained that cash flow was suffering because invoices were being sent up to a month late, and some debtors were not being chased until a year after payment was due. I didn't point the finger of blame at anyone, but gave them the figures for the interest we had paid in the last year on the loans to cover overdue accounts. They were surprised and concerned at the amount. I then asked them to think of some office systems which could prevent this happening in the future. We had quite a good problem-solving meeting. Everyone had ideas on what had caused the problem and on systems which could solve it. In the end we allocated responsibility for a block of accounts to each member of staff, and agreed to have short monthly meetings for reporting on the state of each person's accounts. Very few problems surfaced after that. Because we handled it this way, everyone was creative and constructive about ways of solving the problem. They also thought of solutions which would not have occurred to me on my own.

One advantage of the pull strategy is that it uses the other person's ideas. This wins their commitment and enriches the final decision. Two heads are better than one. The other advantage is that it develops the other person's ability to work out solutions to problems and make decisions.

There are disadvantages in using the pull strategy all the time:

1. it is inappropriate when quick or routine decisions have to be made; and
2. if you always use it you run the risk of being seen as weak and indecisive.

However, it would also be a mistake to use push all the time because your subordinates won't develop and you may be seen as arrogant and draconian. Powerful, effective managers use pull frequently, but use their judgement about the circumstances. They know that many people actually require a more directive push style of influence, and you need to put yourself into these people's shoes to see how they may be feeling about the situation.

Getting your timing right

Influence is not just a matter of deciding on your approach; you also need to sort out your timing. Jerry Stockbridge has a well-polished strategy which relies on the careful timing of each stage.

> I often had to approach the British Telecom authority boards over important decisions such as computerising directory enquiries or modernising phone boxes. My strategy is based on the knowledge that people don't like getting things cold. I have developed a three-stage system. First, I present the overall proposition and get the board to agree that it's a good idea. I then ask the board to note the strategy and to comment. Three months later I do my second stage. I send the board a tactics paper which says: you have agreed the strategy; here are the tactics; here are my proposals on the timings for implementation. I describe the critical paths. I ask the board to note this. I never suggest alternatives, just get my proposals minuted. Later on I go back to the board for stage three. At this stage I say: you've agreed my strategies and tactics; and I refer to the minutes. I then ask them to approve resources and spending on the proposal to which they have already given agreement.
>
> This approach has never failed me. Ultimately the crucial thing is to get resource approval. Of course, I only use this strategy when my proposals are about company goals that have already been agreed upon. If you try to get a decision to spend money at the first meeting they will want to examine your strategy and tactics anyway. If you're managing this through your boss (if he is doing the presentation), then you have to do a big briefing job and it may fail.

Having sorted out your strategy and timing, give a thought to your influence style. There are a number of influence styles you might choose. Think about which of the following you would normally use in the course of your work.

Influence styles

Coerce This is when you insist, or even threaten. It can produce resentment or lack of commitment. On the other hand, if you use it sparingly people will respect you for being strong enough to stand up for yourself in the face of resistance. Take, for example, the case where one of your staff is being persistently poor at timekeeping. You have spoken to her a number of times, tried to find out why she is always late, helped her to think through solutions, but nothing has worked. You may then decide that the time has come for a showdown. A few strong, sharp words, insisting that she complies with office times, and a threat of disciplinary procedures, may help her to see the light, where kindness and patience have failed. However, if you do make threats you must follow through with them if she doesn't respond.

Educate This means providing information or introducing new concepts. People will learn if your information is seen as relevant. You will be distrusted if there is a conflict of interests. This is a valuable style as people often resist if they do not know or understand enough about a proposition. Don't rely on it to work in all cases, however. Resistance is often based on emotions and can be irrational. Then you need to attend to concerns that are deeper than lack of knowledge. Education can work well in overcoming resistance to things that people are frightened of because they don't understand them. Computers are a good example.

Sell This is about emphasising the benefit of your suggestions. Make sure you focus on the benefits that the other person is interested in. Enthusiasm will help you to sell, but no one likes an oversell. People like to be given a chance to think things through for themselves. Tony Hughes used selling to gain acceptance from Whitbread for the investment in TGI Fridays. He researched the position well and worked out a clear vision of the future, then approached his sponsors with great enthusiasm and *sold* them the idea.

Rational/Logical This means presenting an argument based on logic and reasoning. Obviously you won't influence if you are illogical, but remember that people aren't always rational in their decision-making. This style will fail if there is a conflict of interests. It requires a low emotional temperature. This style is an important part of most attempts to influence. Used on its own, it is unlikely to be effective unless the other person is unthreatened and unpressurised, and can sit back and be objective.

Emotive Here you appeal to feelings and values. It often involves making people feel guilty. It can be counterproductive if people suspect you of using emotional blackmail. A trusted manager can successfully appeal to people's emotions to get them to put a big effort into a cause, if they also feel that the cause is worthwhile. Sales managers, for example, often rally their salespeople to achieve particularly high sales targets just before the end of the financial year, so that the annual budget can be reached or exceeded.

Expert This is where you use superior knowledge or expertise. You need to be credible to use this style. It certainly gives you influence if you can quote new information that other people don't have and question assumptions. You can't be easily challenged. Just being the expert doesn't give you influence, you've got to *use* your expertise. You can be very influential if you use your knowledge to shape events, and develop new policies and practices. Even if you don't have the expertise yourself, you can use your contacts with experts outside the company to give you knowledge and therefore credibility. Remember there is a danger of dependence, and of becoming the scapegoat if the solution does not work.

I have seen this influence style used very effectively in meetings. The person with the expertise sits quietly at the start, while the others grapple with the task. The expert's entry into the discussion is timed to coincide with the point of maximum frustration. He or she then quietly but confidently analyses the situation, produces relevant facts and steers a way forward. There is no need to claim that one is an expert (that puts people off); knowledge and reputation are all that are necessary to establish influence in a meeting where the others are a bit lost.

Model This means demonstrating the desired way of behaving. It can be effective if you are very impressive and are around long enough for people to copy you. An effective senior manager, with good people skills, can, through modelling, train the managers under him or her. Do as I do, is, in this case, much more effective than do as I say.

Charisma Charismatic people use their personality and ego strength. You have to have a good supply of charm and personal power to use this. People can feel manipulated if you overdo it. Sometimes, however, charisma can get a reluctant subordinate to act, where hours of persuasion and logic from a po-faced boss would fail.

Negotiate Very often people try to work towards a negotiated outcome which will satisfy at least some of each party's interests. This requires some compromise, so you may not get everything you want, but it is often the only realistic way forward. When you show that you are willing to give a little it increases listening and debate, reduces defensiveness and makes a satisfactory outcome more likely. Successful negotiations depend on having tolerance and respect, even for others to whom you are not particularly close. It means you need to believe that the other person's ideas, opinions and concerns, even if different from your own, should not be peremptorily dismissed.

Negotiation should be used in business a lot more than it is. It can be particularly useful when you are dealing with other departments over whom you have no authority, and where long-term relationships are important.

Joint problem-solving This is about mutual agreement of the best decision. It requires a high level of trust, but can lead to a good decision and to high commitment. It is, however, time-consuming and unsuitable for everyday, routine matters. For example, if you have a subordinate who is consistently performing under par, involving him in finding a way to improve the situation is more likely to work than simply ordering a change. If you manage to get an open discussion going, you may find that there are things that you, as his manager, can do to help the situation improve. Chances are that you will find a more workable solution than if you just thought about it on your own, and then told him what to do.

Non-directive With this style you encourage the other person to develop their own analysis of and solutions to the problem. This leads to the highest possible commitment of the other person to the solution, but you have less control over the nature of the solution. A non-directive style can be very useful when you suspect that a person has work problems that are caused or exacerbated by personal problems.

Now think about the styles which you use and see what they tell you about yourself. If you always prefer to use a 'pull' strategy and influence styles like 'educate', 'joint problem-solving' and 'non-directive', then that may reflect the type of job you have, but it also says something about your personality and about the sort of relationships you prefer to have with other people. You obviously prefer to share the decision-making with others rather than to be directive. You will be seen as a democratic manager, but if you overuse these approaches you may be seen as indecisive.

If, on the other hand, you prefer the 'push' strategy and choose influence styles such as 'coerce', 'sell', 'expert', 'model' and 'charisma', then you may be the sort of personality who prefers to lead from the front. People may see you as a strong leader, but if this is overdone they may also see you as domineering. Excessive use of the 'push' strategy will stifle growth in your subordinates, because it will limit their opportunities to learn from joining in with decision-making.

It helps to become aware of your preference because if you have a tendency to use the same strategy and style with everyone your success rate may not be high. What influences one person can often fail with another. For example, the use of expertise as a way of influencing works with some people and in some professions, but not in others. Even doctors who used to be able to rely on their expertise as an effective influence style, now find that a well-informed patient will sometimes challenge that expertise. You have to learn to judge which style would be most successful and use it. You will learn from trial and error, but you will make fewer mistakes if you try to put yourself in the other person's shoes. Some influence styles may not fit with your personality or your job, but the longer the list of styles in your repertoire, the more likely you will be to choose the style that matches the situation and brings success.[2]

Put yourself into the other person's shoes

Choosing a style and strategy that will work is very much about putting yourself in the other person's shoes. Remember, the person you are trying to influence is as much subject to the pressures of everyday life as you are. It will help if you see influence as a mutual, two-way affair, made more effective by an attempt to understand the other person and the pressures they are experiencing.

To put yourself into the other person's shoes ask yourself the following questions.

- What are this person's concerns about status? Will he worry about losing face? Can I help her to enhance her status?
- Can this person influence those who will make the final decision or whose co-operation we need? Does he or she have the right contacts, or do we need help from someone else?
- Is this person honest, open and straightforward? Can I trust her to say what she thinks and to stick by her agreements? Does he trust me or do I need to prove myself?
- Does this person have anxieties that I need to alleviate?

- Is this person a risk taker, or does he or she need to play it safe and cautiously?
- Does this person need some confidence-building support or training before taking the steps I propose?

When *you* next have to influence someone, do a bit of preplanning: get your facts together and prepare your case. This will make you more self-confident and credible. Then put yourself in the other person's shoes and choose the strategy (push or pull) and the influence style which is most likely to get through to them. Be alert during your meeting, try to think about how they are reacting and whether your approach is working. Ask them what they think of your proposals and be prepared to change your approach if necessary. This sort of sensitivity to the other person will help you to become more skilful.[2]

Getting out: leaving the other person genuinely influenced

The big question at this final stage is – will the person you have influenced actually do what they have agreed to do? They may come under pressure from other people, or they may forget or not find the time to do what they have promised you they will do. Persistence is often required at this stage. People need to be reminded, given deadlines and reinfluenced in one way or another. And, most important, they need to be thanked when they have done it.

In a computer company where I worked as a consultant for a time, getting out and leaving the other person successfully influenced was a problem for the bright young people who worked there. They would go along and present to department managers, who listened sympathet-ically to their ideas and agreed to their proposals. However, these busy managers did with the proposals exactly what they did with everything else that wasn't a priority need for their department, they put it at the bottom of their in-tray and forgot about it.

The clever but naïve young people would wait in vain for the person they had tried to influence to take action. They felt bitter and frustrated when time after time they got no results. A more switched-on person would not have left it at just one meeting, but would have persistently returned to the departmental manager to check on progress, minuted other influential people on the decision, and chased and checked regularly, involving his or her boss, or another senior person in the process to strengthen his or her position. It is easy for non-urgent matters to be neglected, and the switched-on manager would make sure that this could not be the fate of his or her proposal.

If you are influenced in a positive way, you will consider yourself motivated, if not you may feel yourself manipulated. Politics is nothing more than getting what you want done, preferably with the full permission and approval of the others around you. Although you will increase your success rate by polishing up your influence skills, you won't be successful one hundred per cent of the time. It is important to register failure without losing face and making enemies. Don't leave yourself in a position where you have to leave or get a transfer because you've lost so much face. An influential manager needs to be influential all the time, and this includes being influential when you've lost a battle!

To summarise: to get things done at work a manager needs to:

- influence other people by getting involved in the informal power groupings which exist in organisations;
- use skilful behaviour strategies;
- overcome any distaste which may be felt for organisation politics;
- recognise politics as a legitimate way of getting things done and being effective;
- be sensitive to the other person and work out what they want or what they are worried about;
- find an approach which takes these into account; and
- plan out an approach.

Find ways of joining appropriate networks and see how your contacts and influence skills ease the problems that other, less influential people face. You'll find it easier to get resources, defend your important projects and get co-operation from outside your department. And you can achieve all of this without becoming a creep or a manipulative politician!

MAKING YOURSELF POWERFUL

If you want to make yourself powerful, you *can* do it, once you know what to do. As long as you're not incompetent, technically out of your depth or untrained, if you learn the rules and the ropes you can make yourself much more powerful than you are now.

LOOKING TO THE TOP

The first thing to grasp is that you don't get powerful just by being good at your job. Usually that is a prerequisite, but it is never enough. Being clever and competent in a results-orientated company may get you up the first few rungs of the ladder, but thereafter you need to be political and strategic. 'It's a shock when you come from university to learn that you don't just get on by innate ability.'

Take a long look at the senior managers in your organisation and ask yourself, 'What is it that makes these people high status?' Most of the managers I interviewed did just that at an early stage in their careers. And what they saw didn't put them off. 'When I looked at the senior people in my company I realised that they didn't get it right any more often than I did,' says Mike Dearden. 'Their power was certainly not about getting it right one hundred per cent of the time – it was the confidence they had in simply taking and using the power. Us younger managers were reticent about assuming power. That was the main difference. Getting powerful is partly about ability, but it's more about personal drive. It was nice when I realised that I didn't need to be perfect in order to be powerful.'

If gaining power and status isn't about being right all the time, then what is it about? It's about the following:

- being clear about what you want;
- getting started from a power base;
- getting a sponsor and building alliances;
- ensuring that things happen;
- acquiring credibility;
- helping other people;
- getting benefits for your group;
- giving direction;
- earning authority and deference;
- starting new projects.

BEING CLEAR ABOUT WHAT YOU WANT

In order to be powerful you've got to be clear about what you want, and you've got to work single-mindedly to achieve that goal. Jerry Stockbridge has this to say about it:

> Things are much easier when you're clear about what you want. It is easy to be powerful when you're single-minded about your goal, because who can help you and how becomes clear once *you* are clear about what you're aiming for. Power is directing energy to achieve a goal, so when you know what you want you're more effective.
>
> I haven't always been able to apply this. When I am gripped with indecision, boredom or uncertainty and have no sense of purpose then it doesn't happen. When I find myself in this position I back out and let the issues sort themselves out, and come back into play when my way ahead becomes clear again. It's very hard to do anything about increasing my power during a reorganisation, it just doesn't suit me, I lose my clarity and purpose. Impending reorganisations make people introspective and it blocks initiative.

Like Jerry I have also found that I have made the biggest gains in increasing my power when I have been clear and enthusiastic about my goals. Even if becoming chairman of a major multinational is not a realistic ambition for you, it is still worthwhile to set goals. If what you want out of life is simply a rewarding and stimulating job, then you still have to plan for it. Everyone I interviewed confirmed that you don't get anywhere worth while unless you plan for it. Identifying what you want out of life, and then systematically planning how to achieve it is necessary for everybody. It is those people who don't set goals who drift around and find themselves either powerless or doing things they don't enjoy.

Setting goals

To help clear your mind about what you're aiming for try doing the following exercise on goal setting and action planning. Just remember, an important first stage in setting achievable goals is self-knowledge; you must be realistic (but not unduly modest) about your capabilities.

EXERCISE

Stage One

To start the planning process it is useful to decide what it is you want out of life. Picture yourself five years into the future. Think of how you would like to be then in some detail.

- Where are you living?
- What does your house/flat look like?
- What does it cost (in today's prices)?
- Who are you living with?
- What work are you doing?
- What do you earn?
- What are your achievements?

To help you do this well, close your eyes and see yourself at home, and at work. Try to imagine what you are wearing, how senior you are and your relationship with the people around you. When you have done this think of three words that express the sorts of things you are aiming for in your life and hope to achieve in the next five years. Write these words down. These three words won't provide you with specific, concrete goals, but they will give you a good start in working out what you want out of life, and what sort of goals you should be setting. When you have done this you are ready to move on to the second stage of the exercise.

When you do Stage Two of this exercise it is worth considering your personal goals as well as work-related goals, because they do impinge on each other. Remember, to avoid stagnation, make sure to set new goals when you have achieved the first batch. You'll be surprised at how quickly you do achieve your goals and increase your power once you have done this sort of exercise.

Stage Two
Using the chart opposite you can draw up plans for achieving what you want out of life. The chart encourages you to decide on specific activities to achieve your goals and target dates. When you are setting your goals use this checklist as a guide to ensure that they are realistic and achievable.

1. Make it *specific* rather than general. For example, say you want to increase sales of x by 20 per cent within the next three months, rather than simply – and vaguely – to be better at selling.
2. Is it geared towards *action*? That is, what will I be *doing* in working towards my goal?
3. Is it *realistic*? Is it truly attainable or am I setting my aim too high? (Several) small goals are more attainable and therefore more likely to be successful.
4. To what extent am I fully *involved* with the goal? Or is its achievement dependent on a number of other people?

Action planning is not a magic formula for achieving power goals, but it does help you to make important decisions about your life. You may find when you are setting goals that there are some immovable obstacles either at work or in your personal life. Doing this exercise will help you to decide things like whether a change of job, or even your career, is needed.

ACTION PLANNING CHART

Goal	Activities	Helping Forces	Hindering Forces	How Can I Increase the Helping Forces?	How Can I Reduce the Hindering Forces?	Target Date
(What do I want to achieve?)	(What will I be doing in working towards my goal?)	(What or who will help me reach my goal?) (List)	(What or who will hinder me reaching my goal?) (List)	(List)	(List)	**Reality Check** Is it all worth it? If not, review your original goal

When you have completed the action planning chart you need to make sure that you actually do the things you have planned. The best way of ensuring this is to discuss your ideas with another person whom you trust, and fix a date on which you are going to report to them that you have taken the steps on your action plan.

Take a look at the way John Nicholas used goal setting and planning to increase his power. In 1977 he was headhunted to join Condé Nast and National Magazine and moved from the brewery industry into the world of magazine publishing and distribution. He decided that he wanted a top position in this industry and he had to plan how to achieve this goal.

The first eighteen months were hard because I had to make my mark at a senior level but as an ignorant newcomer. I had to achieve first of all in areas that didn't need publishing expertise, because I didn't have it yet. My opportunity to shine and acquire real confidence came during a major transport strike. My office became like Churchill's operations room in the Second World War. As a result of herculean efforts we got our books and magazines to the outlets more successfully than any of our competition.

After that I went through a casualty-strewn but catalystic period. We lost a big US client; a lot of new managers were brought in and ultimately my face didn't fit. With my long-term goal in mind, I decided to take an area of publishing that other people didn't know much about, and become an expert at that. So I decided to develop an expertise in international circulation. I started this at Condé Nast and became a publishing consultant specialising in distribution and subscriptions.

While consulting I learned the game of publishing more thoroughly. One of my big projects was to launch *BBC Wildlife* magazine. In 1983 I became the managing director of The Director Publications. By then I was able to combine both business experience and publishing completely, so I not only filled the job, but was able to do a professional job to lift the magazine. In 1985 I became deputy director general of the Institute of Directors, and still retained the publishing responsibility as chairman.

John didn't let the problems of new management at Condé Nast discourage him. He had a clear goal, and because he knew what he wanted he was able to find another route to achieving it.

Jerry Stockbridge also has a success story to relate, which starts with having some very clear and strong career goals. He knew what he wanted right from the outset, so that made him succeed in persuading the Post Office to give him a position which provided him with good management experience. This choice of job set the pattern for his future advancement.

When I completed my education and had become a chartered engineer and done a post-graduate course in acoustics, I decided I wasn't into decibels, but wanted to go into management. With this in mind I persuaded the Post Office, against their will, to put me into a local area manager post. Normally they preferred to put graduates into head office.

I was lucky – I hit upon some people who were willing to let me do what I wanted. I was fairly persuasive because I said that an area manager job was the only one that I wanted. I was very clear about what I wanted to do, and this helped me to influence them. In fact I remember saying, 'This is what I want, how are we going to achieve it?' I found that when I put it that way, people immediately started working on the 'how' rather than on the 'if'. After a few other postings at which I learnt useful skills such as trade union negotiating, working out strategies, file keeping and preparing briefs, I decided that I wanted to widen my exposure within the company to non-technical grades. (I had come up the technical grade route.) So to achieve this I decided to aim at becoming an area general manager. I judged all my job offers against this criterion; were they steps to an area general manager's job?

After a couple of posts which were useful stepping-stones towards my goal, I was offered a job as principle private secretary to the new chairman who came from outside of the Post Office. This didn't look like a move towards an area general manager job but I liked him and decided to give it a try. But I took the job on the condition that it would last for two years and then I would become an area general manager. Finally, in 1979, at the age of 35, I achieved my lifetime goal, and became the area general manager of the West London telephone area.

In the 1980s Jerry continued to be given good jobs, but he no longer had a clear, burning career goal. He felt during this period that British Telecom (as it became in 1980) had lost its way, and was forever reorganising. He felt that the constant reorganisations disempowered not just him, but everyone else. In 1988 he got an attractive job in the overseas division which involved him in pioneering and creating new business. He feels this is not as powerful a position as the others were, because it is not what British Telecom's main business is about. However because it is about innovation it does give him the chance to be noticed.

GETTING STARTED FROM A POWER BASE

It is an important truth that if you want to make yourself more powerful you do need to keep to the mainstream, to stick with the core business of your organisation. It is here that the main decision-makers reside, and it is from these mainstream jobs that most top people make it to the board. If you do accept jobs in peripheral areas such as personnel or quality control, make sure that you only stay there for a limited time, and use it as a way of gathering information on how the whole business works.

To achieve more power people generally move *from* a power base. For example, in multinationals the home power base is often the strongest. It is within these central power bases that you build your alliances with the decision-makers. Young people who are trying to get more power should go for jobs that are near to the current seats of power; PA positions are a good example. If you're trying to increase your power within a company it is very difficult to do it from the sidelines.

GETTING SPONSORS AND BUILDING ALLIANCES

The most useful thing you can do, if you want to make yourself more powerful, is to get a sponsor. Nobody makes it into jobs without a senior, powerful sponsor who can:

- give them opportunities to prove themselves;
- put their name forward for good jobs; and
- defend them when they've made a mistake.

Remember, if you live by performance, you die by performance. If you depend on rising up and maintaining your position just by being a good performer then you'll come a cropper sooner or later, and without a sponsor to defend you and give you a chance, you soon can find yourself put out to grass. No one can guarantee to maintain high performance consistently. Everyone makes mistakes, and even if, by some miracle, you don't, then a down turn in the market could ruin your results through no fault of your own.

Performance may be enough lower down, especially in companies that have more of a results culture than a power culture. But as you get nearer to the top, even in these companies, you begin to need allies. As Martin Smith says, no one can depend on always being right. Nearer to the top the air is thinner, and your mistakes are very much more obvious. Without powerful friends to back you, one of those mistakes could be your undoing. Even if the mistake or poor result isn't bad enough to justify your demise, it can be used politically by a colleague who has his eye on your empire.

Ally building is not just a defensive strategy; sponsors will also help you in a positive way, to progress your career. You don't need to be a genius to make it to the top in many organisations. If you're good at getting sponsors, then you only need to be competent, not amazingly clever. Jim Davies's story of how he came to hold a senior job in Saatchis is all about making friends and getting sponsors.

I've never been the most brilliant account man, but you don't need to be. You've got to make friends in the right places. Clients don't necessarily want very intelligent people, they want people to whom they can relate. I took a year off when I was 30 and ended up in Australia. My marriage had broken up so I negotiated a year off with Saatchis where I had been an account director on the Schweppes account. I kept running out of money in Australia so I took a job in an advertising agency just to get the money to travel back to London. While I was working I met a contact from

Schweppes at a dinner party, who was there with his British Airways client. Through this chance meeting I learnt that Saatchis were getting the BA account. I rang Saatchis to discuss it and ended up setting up an agency in Sydney to run the Australian end of this account. I ran this agency for four or five years, and while doing so was close to an Australian called Bill Muirhead who was the group account director at Saatchis in London in charge of the BA account. We became friends. Bill Muirhead then became chairman of Saatchis' London office and started putting me under pressure to come back to the heart of it all. In 1988 I came back and am now one of the chief operating officers running a quarter of the agency's billing.

How to acquire sponsors

Sponsors will help you if they believe in you, even if you don't directly ask them to. But first they must get to know you, so networking is essential. The first step in building the sort of network you will need if you are going to acquire powerful sponsors is to ask yourself, 'What is my network like now? Do I spend enough of my time meeting and communicating with powerful people?'

One good way of clarifying your present position is to draw a communications map like the one on page 64. Put yourself in the middle, then put all the people you communicate with in a circle around you. Draw thick black lines from your central position to the people with whom you communicate most frequently, and dotted lines to those with whom you have less contact.

Finally, underline all the powerful people on your map, then you will see quite easily whether you spend most of your time with powerful or less powerful people.

Communications map

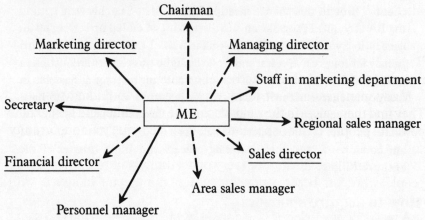

The person in the middle in this example is a marketing manager. You can see at a glance that he is not devoting enough time to building powerful allies. He is spending a lot of time with his drinking crony, the regional sales manager, and also with his secretary. The only board member he sees at all frequently is his boss, the marketing director.

If you find yourself in this position, work out a strategy for increasing your contacts with senior people. In some cases, you may simply need to break the comfortable habit of spending time only with junior people. In other cases, the job may not provide enough opportunities for you to interact with senior people. Then you have to get creative. Get yourself on important projects if you can, even little ones like organising a meeting for senior people. Things like this give you visibility, although they often involve you in long hours. The next time a consultant comes to investigate and recommends changes to your department, try to attach yourself to him as the internal person helping with the investigation. Often the person who works with the consultant gets the job of implementing the recommendations and running the department after the consultant goes. Consultants often have the ear of senior people. If they find you helpful and competent they will mention you in the circles where promotion decisions are made.

Jerry Stockbridge found that working with trade unions supplied him with good opportunities for getting known in the right circles. 'In 1970 I got an opportunity to negotiate pay and conditions with the trade unions in the Post Office. This exposed me to the national leaders of all the unions. They in turn spent time with the senior managers in the organisation, including the chairman (and also with the prime minister when a labour government was in power).'

In order to get sponsors in a multinational company you need to spend time in the head office, wherever in the world that may be. Remember that your sponsors will need to use the same lavatories and restaurants as the chairman and chief executive.

Many managers are just lucky when it comes to finding sponsors. They find themselves in the right place at the right time, and get to know powerful people. If this happens to you then recognise your opportunity and go for it. However, if luck doesn't come to you then you'll just have to go out and look for it. Use every opportunity you can to work with people who can become your sponsors or put you in touch with sponsors.

A really clever trick is to find a sponsor who is a fast-stream rising star and be pulled up to the top with him or her. However, you can't expect always to pick the right one. If your sponsor leaves the organisation or falls from favour, you may find the same thing happening to you. Beware of what can happen to you if you lose a sponsor and fail to replace him or her.

> One of my colleagues became chairman of a subsidiary company. He had a senior sponsor at head office. My colleague was very nice, in fact he was the best-liked senior executive in the organisation, but he was not very political. His head office sponsor lost his job and then he was in trouble. My colleague's boss did not like his management style, and as soon as the sponsor was no longer there to protect my friend, the boss started to attack. He quickly broke up my colleague's empire. As his staff realised that he was in trouble they began to leave. Within nine months three-quarters of them had gone. So my friend had to leave and start his own business.

A strategic person will be selective when choosing a sponsor. The right sponsor will help you upwards much more quickly. It is important not to hitch yourself to a sponsor who is going nowhere. Don't work for a no-hoper who does nothing for you; pick an achiever. Get to know who the achievers are by working on jobs or projects with them. Don't surround yourself with people who aren't good, try to work with good people who stretch you. The jobs that stretch you, the ones that you're not sure you can do, are the ones that make you. If you can trust the people around you you can just go in to the difficult jobs and then do them.

Don't make the mistake of modestly thinking that it is an imposition to expect some senior person to put time and energy into becoming your sponsor. Senior managers are there to help promising junior people to succeed. Indeed, if you do well with the help of your sponsor it will reflect well on him or her. Colleagues will see that he or she is exercising good judgement in people.

Mentors

Mentors are slightly different from sponsors. They are people, usually wise and quite senior, to whom you can turn for advice. They don't necessarily provide you with the opportunities that a sponsor can, but their advice and inside knowledge can help you to make the right career decisions. Try to have both, you need all the help you can get!

The importance of having good personal relationships

You won't attract sponsors just by being good at your job, you must take the trouble to make friends with people. Impressing people about how clever you are works against you if you don't have good personal relationships. Be consistent with your views and your attitudes towards people. This will make you more trustworthy and you will find it easier to build alliances.

ACQUIRING CREDIBILITY

The credibility you need for becoming more powerful comes from many sources. You can gain credibility by having a reputation for competence or technical expertise. But make sure that this expertise is in an area that is important for the growth of the company, otherwise it won't work so well for you. It's probably more important to avoid having a reputation for incompetence. Credibility is also acquired by knowing the rules of the game, and responding to the expectations and values of your followers. You've got to fit in and yet be different enough (hopefully in a positive way) to get noticed and acquire a reputation.

You also need to build your credibility through action – giving advice, influencing others, having presence, making projects work – all of these things will build your reputation. This demands of you a capacity to approach relationships and problems in terms of the present rather than the past. It also demands that you are able to get on and *do* things, without constant approval and recognition from others. Most of all, credibility is earned by people who get jobs done and who solve problems. Lower down in organisations, managers get noticed for their persistence and single-mindedness. People who leap over obstacles and drive through walls in a focused way do build good reputations. Higher up the ladder the rules change, and if you're interested in increasing your power and moving beyond first-line management, then you've got to pay attention to these subtle changes. As people get more senior they are required to 'smooth out', to become more balanced, to round off the rough edges and to treat others more gently. You are still expected to get results, but through the skilful management of your team, rather than by bulldozing your way through.

It can be difficult for introspective people to build credibility. If you don't want to speak up unless you're sure of the facts, and if you're in the habit of expressing your feelings before stating opinions or solutions, then this could hinder you. Training courses in assertion, influence and confidence building will help in cases like these.

HELPING OTHER PEOPLE

It is interesting to see from studies of all sorts of communities that one of the things that characterises high-status people is the fact that they are active in giving help and advice to others. Sponsoring others is a way of being powerful, you help people with their personal development.

High-status people establish and maintain their power by being responsive to requests for their help and time, and for their social and technical skills. This of course leads to reciprocity, so that high-status people, through their generosity, end up helping themselves. They also have the energy and perseverance to keep circulating among their followers. As a result they become natural data banks and others turn to them for up-to-date information.

GETTING BENEFITS FOR YOUR GROUP

Nothing legitimates and establishes your power more than your ability to handle external relations for your group. Research done on what makes managers popular confirms this. Those managers who are nice are not the most popular. The prize goes to the managers who have the most power to acquire benefits for their subordinates. As you build your reputation as an effective link for your group with the world outside (top management, other departments, customers, suppliers etc), so you establish yourself as a leader.

Respected leaders manage external relations for their group very effectively and bring back benefits, information and protection. Even bad-tempered bosses who win fights for their groups end up being loved by them. Managing group boundaries with the outside world includes:

- getting unreasonable demands modified;
- defending subordinates from the justified or unjustified consequences of their mistakes;
- defending subordinates from interference with their schedules;
- getting resources and permission to do things from top management;
- getting timely information (before it comes through on the grapevine).

To achieve these benefits for your group you need to become a powerful, articulate, patient and persistent advocate. You need to be skilful at both formal presentations and at informal influencing and politics.

GIVING DIRECTION

Being able to give clear direction is a consequence of circulating among your followers and your colleagues and becoming a mine of information. Use this information to give direction, to advise courses of action, to warn against dangerous people or activities – all of this builds up your reputation as a sensible and wise leader. Even when you don't know the answer you need to be able to direct the enquirer towards someone who does.

EARNING AUTHORITY AND DEFERENCE

A manager who wants to become more powerful must earn authority and deference. The ability to command and to expect and get responsiveness is a basic leadership requirement. To gain in power, people must perceive that you have authority. This doesn't mean that you have to manage with an authoritative, directive style. But you do need to behave in such a way that people see you as having authority, even if you prefer to reach decisions by consensus.

To exercise authority managers must:

- motivate their subordinates to accept orders and/or requests;
- gain credibility as a legitimate source of authority; and
- cope with confrontations when orders are ignored or disputed.

The skills you need for achieving authority are described in detail in Chapter 9.

STARTING NEW PROJECTS

Tasks that are capable of being made routine, predictable and regulated have less power associated with them. If your job can be minutely measured and regulated, there is little scope for making yourself more powerful through it. If you want to be powerful, you've got to avoid jobs where you will be taken for granted, and treated like a low-status service group that jumps to respond when asked. You need to demonstrate that your work is unpredictable and difficult for an outsider to schedule, specify or cost.[4]

A very good way of making sure you're not stuck and typecast doing routine work is to get involved as much as possible in innovations. The first time a new activity is performed, or any new technology installed, it appears extraordinary and worthy of high status. Once the innovation is perfected and routinised, it becomes downgraded in the eyes of top management. Fast-track people are attracted to newly created jobs, because that's how they increase their visibility. Paradoxically, the success of a project or function makes it less possible for the people running it to gain credibility as successful individuals. It is the trailblazers struggling with new and difficult problems who attract the attention of top management.

Ambitious people find that it pays to:

- innovate;
- get approval for new projects; and
- sell customers on a new product they hope to be able to acquire or develop.

Tony Hughes is one of the trailblazers. While he was operations director at Beefeater, the company went through an exciting period where they opened a new steakhouse every eight days for two years. In 1985 he spotted TGI Fridays (a lively, young persons' restaurant chain) in the US. He initiated the development of TGI Fridays in the UK through franchises.

This proved a big commercial success and in 1990 he was given the job of transferring the best practices from TGI Fridays to the rest of the Whitbread restaurant business.

> We achieved a level of customer service in TGI Fridays not seen in Whitbread before. Now I am standards director for the restaurant division of Whitbread. I'm always doing new things – starting new projects. Once it's routinised it's no fun. I'm predisposed towards trailblazing. I have enthusiasm and energy for getting things going. I don't necessarily want to be the biggest, but I do want to be the best. This is not the norm in Whitbread where there is an element of compliance, as you would expect in any big company.

In spite of the fact that such enthusiastic trailblazing has not been the norm in Whitbread, Tony has reached his current position as a direct result of his successful new projects.

Work in the critical areas if you can

Even if you can't get involved in new projects, it pays to work in areas of the company that are seen as critical to organisational success, because they are less predictable and routinised. The moral for the young manager in search of power to remember is this. Move into critical functional areas and then move out at the right time.

If you are stuck in a department where the work is low or medium status, thus reducing your power, here are some things you can try:

- seek to professionalise your work so that only you and your colleagues (with special training and experience) can understand many of the problems involved;
- rid your area of routine service activities;
- take on activities that make your work more irregular;
- add functions to your job that put you in a position where you are appraising the work of other departments;
- seek to shift your department to an earlier stage in the decision chain for new projects; and

- add research or innovative tasks which are difficult for outsiders to evaluate and which increase your autonomy.[4]

Building up your power takes time and effort, and for most of us there is no magic short cut, but it *is* open to anyone who is willing to take the necessary steps. It is a great shame to see talented, hard-working people, who through their political naïvety, never become powerful or influential, and then become switched off and cynical about their organisation. There is a pattern to the career histories of such people, and it looks something like this.

- At the beginning there is an enthusiastic young manager or professional who tries hard to be competent and to improve their company's service to its customers.
- He or she is so interested in the job that any other activity, such as networking or career planning, is seen as an irrelevant irritant.
- They eventually find, as their responsibilities increase, that time must be spent vying for resources to get the job done. Disliking political activity and finding it a distraction, they do it badly and frequently fail to get what they want.
- They then develop negative attitudes towards the more politically astute managers who often succeed where they fail to get either resources or promotion.
- They see politically active and successful people as wasting time that could be better spent on getting on with the job.
- They prefer to mix with other people with similar problems, so their attitudes harden.
- These attitudes appear cynical and politically immature to senior managers. They therefore don't build alliances, don't get sponsored, and don't get powerful.

If you want to get on, don't become one of these!

Now complete the following questionnaire to assess your current situation. The questions are designed to help you think about the sources of power you have.

MEASURE YOUR CURRENT POWER[5]

1. Position power

(a) Do you have the formal right to make decisions, other than trivial ones (particularly decisions that involve the expenditure of large sums of money)?

(b) Do other people need your approval before they take any action?

(c) Do you supervise anyone else's work?

(d) Do your decisions significantly affect important aspects of the organisation's work in the long term?

(e) Do your superiors typically support your decisions and not overrule them?

(f) Do you encounter any resistance to your *right* to make decisions/ supervise others/give approval, from subordinates, peers, senior managers?

(g) Do you work in a geographically or functionally peripheral part of the company?

'Yes' answers to any of Questions (a) – (e) indicate your possession of authority.

'Yes' to Question (d) indicates a high level of power based on authority.

'Yes' to Questions (f) and (g) suggests a reduction of your political resources which you may need to do something about.

2. Expertise

(a) Does it take a year or longer to learn to do your job competently?

(b) Do you need qualifications to do your job?

(c) Do you have the highest qualification in your field?

(d) Are you the only person in your organisation who can do your job, or one of the few?

(e) If you were to leave your organisation, would they have difficulty in replacing you?

(f) Does your knowledge and skill relate to the core business of the organisation?

(g) Do people frequently consult you and follow your advice?

(h) Do senior managers clearly show that they value your input?

(i) Are you judged to be particularly competent at what you do by other colleagues?

'Yes' to any of Questions (a) – (h) and (i) indicate your possession of expert power, but 'No' to Questions (g) and (h) suggests a lack of perception of your expertise by others, and you may need to do something about this to ensure that this political resource is fully used.

3. Resource control

(a) Can you give or withhold access to the following resources of your organisation:
 – money?
 – information (non-trivial)?
 – promotion?
 – training?
 – senior managers and other powerful people?
 – computers and other operational or administrative facilities?
 – 'perks'?
 – accommodation?
(b) Are others aware that you can give or withhold access to these things, perhaps because you have, on occasions, refused them?
(c) Do others have alternative sources of access to these resources?

'Yes' to any of the items in Question (a) indicates that you have power based on resource control. 'No' to Question (b) suggests that you may need to do something about this in order to use this political resource fully. 'Yes' to Question (c), with reference to any resource, indicates a low level of power in relation to that resource.

4. Association

(a) Are you on friendly terms with a number of people in your organisation across different departments?
(b) Do you know who the powerful people are, do you know them well, and are you in frequent contact with them?
(c) Do you have connections outside work with some of the more powerful people in your organisation?
(d) Do you socialise over coffee, drinks or meals with people at work?
(e) Do people at more senior level drop in for chats with you in your office, or call you on the phone for chats?
(f) Do you work closely with anyone who is very senior to you in the hierarchy?
(g) Do you have a powerful sponsor?

'Yes' to any of these questions indicates your power is based on your alliances.

5. Interpersonal

(a) Do people confide in you?

(b) Do you usually speak at meetings?

(c) Are you an 'active listener'? Do you make sure you have understood the other person's point of view? Do you make it clear to them that you understand and empathise?

(d) Do you make sure that other people take your views seriously when it matters to you?

(e) Do you avoid being either passive or aggressive in formal or informal discussions with others in the organisation?

(f) Can you hold the attention of a group or larger audience? Can you give a persuasive presentation?

(g) Are you aware that people admire you in some respects, and do others copy you?

(h) Do people want to be with you at informal meetings?

(i) Do people come to you for advice, direction and help?

(j) Are you good at getting resources and information for your group, and at defending them when necessary?

'Yes' to any of these questions indicates your power is based on interpersonal skills.

6. Innovation

(a) Are you frequently involved in new projects?

(b) Is your work seen as critical to the success of the organisation?

(c) Is your work seen as exciting and high status?

(d) Is your work seen as routine and easily measurable?

(e) Is your work seen as a low-status service function?

'Yes' to Questions (a) – (c) means that you are gaining power through being involved in new areas of work, critical to the organisation's success. 'Yes' to Questions (d) and (e) means that your power is limited due to the low-status nature of the functions in which you work.

After the questionnaire

Now that you have assessed your current power, see what opportunities you can find to increase it. No career plan is complete without a plan for increasing your power and influence. Use the following strategies:

- Decide what you want out of life and set clear goals.
- Get sponsors to give you opportunities to show your talents and get promoted.
- Get mentors so that you have a sound source of advice.
- Acquire credibility through positive action in areas critical to the success of the company.
- Increase your status by helping other people, particularly those in your team.
- Behave in a way that earns you authority and deference.
- Get involved in new projects wherever possible. Avoid routinisation.

CHAPTER · 5

ESTABLISHING POWER WHEN YOU'RE NEW TO A JOB

SETTLING IN TO A NEW JOB

How do I establish my leadership and power when I have just started a new job? This is a question that bothers most managers, whether they are changing companies, changing departments, or even moving up a grade in their present department. New opportunities exist in new jobs, both for making your mark *and* for making a fool of yourself. Some companies throw young people in at the deep end in a sink-or-swim challenge. People can flounder in these situations. The first few months are normally hazardous if exciting. Uncertainty and change is in the air; you feel it, and so do your new staff. Uncertainty, newness and ignorance – these are all unsettling and can leave you with a feeling of powerlessness. Power, as we've seen, is not just a question of your actual position or expertise, it's also largely a question of whether or not you are perceived to be powerful. Question marks always hang over the power of a new manager.

- Will she be able to deal with irate customers as well as the last manager did?
- Will he command everyone's respect?
- Will she be approachable?
- Will he know enough about the technicalities of the job to manage the department?

These are just a few of the questions that people will be discussing when you take on your new job.

You won't be able to win everyone over at once, so don't even try. A new manager has gradually to establish his or her leadership and power in the first few months in the office. You will, as a manager, have a certain amount of position power, and you may bring some relevant expertise with you, but as far as your staff are concerned you will have to earn their co-operation and respect in your first few months.

Your main problem will be to avoid giving in to a feeling of being disempowered because of your newness and ignorance. You will also have to guard against a feeling of panic which will incline you to move in and make your presence felt by giving orders, before you have learnt enough about the new job to do this effectively.

There are two ways to ward off those feelings of panic and powerlessness. The first is to remember the strengths you've got and have demonstrated in the past, which got you your new job in the first place. Write them down if you're feeling shaky; a list of your strengths will boost your confidence. Next, plan your strategy for establishing your leadership and power.

FIND OUT WHAT YOU NEED TO KNOW

Your strategy for establishing yourself should start off with finding out what you need to know. This should start at the selection or promotion interview. You need to understand what other people's expectations of you are in the new job. If you aren't told this at the interview, you should ask. Remember, getting more powerful starts with having clear goals. Some of these goals will be your personal goals, but many will be goals that your department or function has to achieve under your leadership, so make sure you know what these are early on.

You will also need to be well informed about such things as:

- the culture;
- values;
- management style;
- the people; and
- the expertise.

Make a plan for how you're going to find out what you need to know about all of these things. Give yourself an agenda for the first three months and set timings. Then you won't be wandering about like a lost soul, and will gain some feelings of power just from having a clear plan and purpose.

The culture

What is the culture of your organisation like? In particular, try to identify the kind of behaviour that is truly valued. It is helpful to find out about the following.

- What size is your organisation?
- How centralised or devolved is the decision-making?
- Is it bureaucratic?
- Is it innovative?
- What is the history of the organisation or department? In particular, what significant events are held in its folklore?
- How is the organisation 'owned'?
- What is the business environment?
- Who are the heroes and heroines or villains? What stories are told about them?
- Are there any rites and rituals?
- Is there a power network? Can you identify the people who form part of it?[6]

Michael Lainas believes that it is important to take the trouble to find out all about the culture when you move to a new job, and to use this knowledge to help you to get established.

The culture is different in every company. You have to identify how decisions are made. In Marketing Solutions there was one very successful, strong person at the top (the founder and chairman), and he gathered information from a number of people around the company. In a situation like this, it is often not enough just to do a good job! It is also necessary to impress a range of target audiences, all of whom will have a view about you when talking to the chairman.

One has to learn about the social structure and culture of the company. You have to recognise what is important to the company and to different groups. In Marketing Solutions there were one or two key people, who were informally rather than hierarchically important. For example, the staff in the accounts department were aware which managers were good at financial controls, and the studio noticed which managers briefed them well, and gave them feedback from the client about their work. The chairman would become aware of all of these views.

When you are new to an organisation you need to be sensitive to the pace at which it can accept change. If the company has been historically very successful the incumbent management will be likely to react adversely to new ideas. You need to think very carefully about the way to influence change without causing irritation.

Values

It's not always easy to find out about values, because it's not the norm for people to talk openly about such things. People do hold values, however, and live by them, whether they talk about them or not. Take the trouble to explore people's values and expectations when you move into a new job. It's very important to share values with your staff, so look for the common ground. When you find differences in values you will have to deal with this, but don't do it in public.

Each of us places a different emphasis on things that are important in our life and work. These values determine how we approach our jobs, so it's as well to be clear about your own values, as well as those held by your new staff. Serious differences will lead to clashes if you try to get people to do things that are counter to their beliefs and values.

On page 80 is a list of some of the things you may value. Think about each item in turn and rate it on a scale of 1 (low) to 10 (high), putting a tick in the appropriate column. When you have worked through the list, add any other values that are especially important to you and rate them too.

Now look at those values which you have rated highly, particularly those for which you have scored 9 or 10. How do those values match those which you feel are valued in your new organisation or department?

If you find it difficult to get people to express their values openly, there are other ways to find out about them. Listen in, as was suggested above in the section on culture, to the folklore of the organisation, and to the stories about heroes, anti-heroes and heroines. This is a good way of picking up clues about what is seen as important.

When I joined PE Consulting Group, this story gave me insight into the values of the company:

A consultant called Peter was part of a team giving a presentation to a client. Peter unfortunately had had too much to drink at lunchtime and disgraced himself when it was his turn to speak. He had somehow got hold of a broom, and used this instead of a microphone. He also presented from the back of the room instead of the front. Apparently his speech was as inadequate as his amplifying equipment. He was quickly escorted off the stage before he could do further damage and locked into

Table of values[6]

	Low 1	2	3	4	5	6	7	8	9	High 10
Leadership										
Status										
Growth										
Achievement										
Risk taking										
Creativity										
Responsibility										
Involvement in decision-making										
Being well organised										
Personal integrity										
Developing knowledge										
Breaking frontiers										
Making money										
Self-respect										
Competition										
Safety										
Security										
Friendship										
Co-operation										
Promotion										
Health										
The environment										
Loyalty										
Being at peace with yourself										
Freedom to take decisions										

the broom cupboard, until the presentation was safely over. The next day he was fired.

I learnt from this story that a consulting company took its clients very seriously, and that presenting a credible image to them was important. Peter's consulting skills were never in question, but his damage to the company image in front of clients was not acceptable. The story told me all I needed to know about those particular values.

You will enhance your power early on by giving significant people whatever fits in with their values. On the other hand, if certain values are very dear to you, and you find that some subordinates on your team don't share these values, then you will have to either negotiate with them, or ask them to leave.

Management style

You will certainly need to know the management style of the outgoing manager. If yours is going to be different, then you may need to begin to make these differences clear quite early on. If, for example, the previous manager was directive and authoritative, and you prefer to make decisions through consensus, then you may have a problem. Your staff will probably expect you to be as directive as the previous boss, and if you try to operate differently there will be some confusion. You will need to explain to everyone what you are going to do that is different, and why this is.

The people

Getting to know the people will be the most important thing you can do. Until you do get to know them they will stereotype you, and this may be counterproductive to your attempts to establish your power. Some managers make the mistake of concentrating on the technicalities of the job and their seniors, and fail to develop relationships with the people who are working for them.

A new manager in a large financial group made this mistake recently. He was recruited from outside to run a department of 120 people. After being in the post for two months he had not spoken to any of his staff other than a few direct reportees. Many of the staff did not know who he was and would not have recognised him if they saw him. He hired a consultant to advise him on how to structure the department. This consultant produced a plan without consulting any of the staff. The result was that the plan made both the manager and consultant look like fools, because the new ideas were not new at all, they were already in existence in the department. Had the manager taken the trouble to get to know some of his staff he would have been put straight before making such a mistake.

Wiser managers realise the importance of getting to know their people. Martin Smith says: 'When I was new at Bankers Trust I spent a lot of time with the individuals. During the first six weeks I had interviews with each of the top twenty people. I got to know what made them tick, and what their problems were. I felt I had to do this to start to develop good personal relationships. I also needed to establish sponsors at head office so I tried to know people there socially as well.'

'When I take on a new job I take a great interest in the people, their views and interests,' says Tony Hughes. 'I get to know the name of each member of staff, and one thing about their personal life that's important to them. This helps me to understand their values. I try to communicate in a fun and exciting way about my approach to the new job. I use this communication not just to get to know people, but to enable them to see the results of their efforts.'

The expertise

Often, in a new job, you will be unfamiliar with the technical expertise, or at least with that aspect of the expertise which is used in that company or department. Learning about the expertise is useful in establishing yourself as a leader, but you must be open about your ignorance at first. When you are new, go and talk to people and take the standpoint – 'I know nothing about all of this, please explain.' You can do this without appearing to be a complete twit. For example, in meetings say little for the first hour, just listen and learn. Then you can intervene effectively later on. Try to ask intelligent questions, and be open about your need to learn.

Remember when John Nicholas joined Condé Nast that he had the problem of being an ignorant, senior outsider? He chose to establish his power in the industry by 'learning the game of publishing more completely than most'.

As you begin to build up a picture of the culture, the people and the expertise, you will be able to make more informed decisions about how best to get yourself accepted as a leader. This knowledge will help you to avoid making some early, damaging mistakes. Also, people will respect you more if they see that you are humble and intelligent enough to make a big effort to learn how to be a good leader to *them*.

GETTING INFORMED BEFORE STARTING THE JOB

Get hold of whatever information you can *before* you start, as this will help you to prepare for establishing leadership and avoiding mistakes which could set you back. If you are already in the company then this will be easier. If it's a new company, try to arrange an informal chat with some of the key people before Day One. Preparing for any disruption to your personal life will also help your initial performance. If you and your family are reeling with the shock of unexpectedly long hours then the strain will tell. If you have to move to another city or country this needs a lot of planning. Don't assume that you can do it all without a lot of help from the company. Disruption to personal life is a frequent cause of low performance from relocating managers.

AVOID EARLY MISTAKES

Here are some mistakes which can be made in the early days, which the managers I interviewed warned against.

Don't try to establish yourself as an expert right away, as you may make yourself unpopular. People will accept your expertise once you have proved yourself in the new company, but not before. 'Be sensitive to your environment,' says Mike Dearden. 'The worst thing you can do is tell people what you've done elsewhere, and then not do it here! When I came to Castrol I was seen as the whiz-kid from outside and I was not welcome. I had to be humble and help people without taking the credit. I still have some alliances today founded on the work I did on those early projects. But if I had been insensitive to their attitude towards outsiders, and had built myself up at their expense, I would have had problems.'

Some managers like to breeze in and take command immediately, establishing their power by ordering people around and daring them to disobey. This doesn't work in many cultures, and the danger is that people may call your bluff and ignore you. Then where are you? As Jerry Stockbridge says, 'I don't think that high-profile giving orders would have worked as an initial strategy. The direct use of power meets with resistance in British Telecom. I had to say – here is what I would like you to do, you don't *have* to do it. I was open with people about the reasons behind the decision and willing to talk it through.'

John Mills has this warning to give. 'When you start a new job, take it easy. People don't yet know you well enough to trust you. It's a great mistake to whiz about setting up projects because you don't have enough to do. After six months people will bring things to you; then you will be very busy. The projects you started at the beginning, you won't be able to follow through.' Remember that power is based on trust, and it takes time to build up this trust. So don't rush it, or else you'll destroy the very power you were hoping to establish.

GAIN STATUS GRADUALLY

Obviously you can't just spend your first three months in a new job learning the ropes. You will have tasks to do, but you will have to work more slowly than you would if you weren't new and learning. There are several ways you can gradually gain status in the early days.

Try setting up a series of meetings and regular events where it is clear that you are running the show. This will get people accustomed to seeing you in a leadership role. Discuss what is happening. Ask for information and suggestions, but give guidance as well, based on your previous experience. Set up good reporting and information systems if they don't already exist. Make sure that you have a good secretary or PA.

Although you shouldn't rush in like a bull in a china shop, you do need to be seen to be a manager who can achieve results. People will be watching to see if you're a man of action, or just a man of activity! Using the information you have gathered about people's expectations, deliver those things early and well. Don't just get it right technically, make sure it looks good too. Remember, people will be judging you in those early days. Also, make sure that you allow others to understand what you can contribute because of your background and experience. The important word to remember is – deliver!

Rosie Faunch advises that you need to deliver early on.

Don't try to change the whole world. Find something quick and easy to do, something that everyone has been complaining about. When I started my present job I was told that the X-ray reports were not getting back into the medical notes. This was extremely difficult for the consultants, who had to see and diagnose patients, and were unable to do so without the X-ray reports. For a very small sum of money I got a clerk in to file the X-rays, and the problem was solved.

It is very important to deal with each individual differently, and to work out ways of relating to that person. This can be crucial in the first few weeks. It is no good treating everyone the same. Try to draw up with each person a list of the things that they have wanted and waited for in the months or years leading up to your appointment. You will probably find that these lists do not add up to a great deal of money, and that you can gain a lot by implementing as many items as possible, quickly.

Most managers advise you to spend a lot of time learning in the first few months rather than to bulldoze your way into power and to risk resistance, unpopularity and mistakes. None the less, they do suggest that you don't wait *too* long before taking decisions and making changes. It's a fine balance, because you don't want to acquire a reputation for being indecisive or inactive. If inaction has been the norm in the past you can quite easily make your name through action and results.

Roger French advises that you make changes relatively quickly. If, when you've gathered your information you see that changes are needed, make them as soon as you can. 'If you don't make changes within a certain period, then it becomes increasingly difficult to do so.' Keith Manning confirms this. 'If within three months you don't know what's going on and you can't make changes, then you've got a problem.'

I am not suggesting that you should move in and make uninformed changes in the first days or weeks just to stamp your authority. People see through and resent such tactics, and will probably resist you. Aim to learn enough about the new job so that you can make well-thought-out changes after you have been there for a few months. Three months seems to be an acceptable amount of time to allow for settling in. Make sure you use this time effectively.

GET CO-OPERATION

You will need to establish your power by getting people accustomed to following your directions. Excessive orders are destructive and oppressive and will harm relationships. But this doesn't mean that the fewer orders you give, the better. People will want and expect you to use your authority once you've learnt what's what. After all, a manager's job is about getting people to do things. Managers need to establish themselves as leaders by actually initiating orders. The trick when you're new is to do it gradually. You move from giving a few orders to giving the right number and frequency. You also give more obvious, easily accepted orders at first, and gradually move to more ambiguous and potentially controversial areas. Get people accustomed to your leadership in less problematic areas, before moving into areas where resistance and argument are likely.

You must also maintain momentum. Your subordinates won't want a string of mindless or needless chores. They will prefer you to respect their ability to get on with the job without constant interference. Yet they won't consider you a leader if you back off and fail to give guidance and instruction where appropriate.

DEALING WITH RESISTANCE

Resistance from subordinates can seriously challenge your leadership status when you're new to your job, and it can lead to a domino effect. Once one person gets away with saying 'no', the others may follow, seeing that you have a chink in your armour. Be careful about challenges to dicey decisions. If you have taken the trouble to learn the culture, values and attitudes of your new staff, the chances are that you will avoid giving orders that will be resisted. However, when you're new, it is easy to make mistakes. If you do meet resistance when you're settling in you need to deal with it, because your reputation as a leader is at stake.

It may be tempting for a new manager to exert his or her authority and simply insist in the face of resistance. This is a high-risk strategy. If you nail your colours to the mast and you still meet point-blank refusal, then you may have to make a difficult choice:

- either you will have to fire the subordinate; or if you can't do that
- you will have to climb down.

It may be safer and more effective to try a 'pull' influence strategy. First, try to establish a common understanding of the nature of the problem and the surrounding constraints. Work towards getting agreement that there is a problem.

Secondly, try to understand the subordinate's values, interests, anxieties and desires. In other words, try to find out what is making him or her want to resist you. If you get such a dialogue going you will create the impression that you are understanding, responsive and interested in their needs. This doesn't necessarily mean you agree with their views, but empathy is always appreciated.

Thirdly, try to redefine the problem in such a way that the subordinate can contribute to the solution. Create a situation where you solve the problem together, with each of you giving some ground. You may not end up with your ideal solution, but at least if you have a workable solution you will have avoided the danger and loss of face of outright refusal to do anything.

If this attempt at negotiating a solution doesn't work then you may have to fire or move him out of your department, although if this person has an essential skill you may be unwise to do this. In this case try to get support from other members of staff, rather than just giving in. People often respond to group pressure when they won't respond to individual pressure.

To summarise, when you're new to a job:

- don't expect to be accepted as the boss easily and immediately;
- work at establishing your power;
- gain acceptance for your right to give orders;
- earn your right to higher status and deference;
- learn the rules of the game – the values, habits and expectations of your new group;
- demonstrate that you have superior ability, either in the technical field or in organising;
- be cautious at first and gradually establish status as you learn what you need to know about your new environment.

CHAPTER 6

INFLUENCING YOUR BOSS

Many managers are comfortable when dealing with people below them in the hierarchy, but not so good at influencing upwards. Influencing senior people, and particularly your boss, is a crucial part of getting on and getting more powerful. An influential, powerful manager manages his or her boss in order to get things done, get resources, and get help and advice. Bosses have access to other senior people, other departments, important outsiders, and most of all, information and experience. Whatever you can't do directly, you will have to do through your boss. Often, he holds the key to your next promotion. So make sure you know how to influence him.

Too many managers say, 'I get on well with my subordinates, we have a strong team, but my boss keeps interfering. I'm getting sick of him,' or 'My boss is a pain – I can never get hold of her or get a decision out of her.' If this is your problem, ask yourself these questions: 'Is it my boss who is the villain, or is it me? Have I learnt all the skills and tactics I need for influencing him and building a good relationship?' If your boss really is the villain, then there is a section at the end of this chapter for dealing with that problem. However, in 90 per cent of cases, the problem can be dramatically reduced if you become more skilful in your management of your boss.

DON'T TRY TO MANIPULATE YOUR BOSS

People often try to manage their bosses through manipulation. So often they say things like:

- 'I've got to work at it to make my boss look good.'
- 'I've got to make my boss think it's *her* idea.'
- 'I've got to convince my boss that this proposal is in *his* interests (when it isn't).'

The trouble with bosses is that they aren't such fools that they don't realise what is happening. Most people (whether they are bosses or not) known when others are playing games with them. It is a mistake on the part of the manipulator to assume that other people are less perceptive than they are. It is not wise to assume that your boss is an idiot and should be manipulated. He or she is a human being. At the very least you should respect, help and keep him informed. Too many people try to undermine their bosses. Eventually, they tend to undermine themselves.

Put yourself in your boss's shoes

Remember, no one has absolute power. Your boss will be constrained by the limits to her power, and may not be able to do what you want every time. In fact, when your boss appears to be rigid or unhelpful, it may be that she is trying to control a situation in which she feels powerless. Try putting yourself in your boss's shoes. The more you understand your boss's pressures, needs and ambitions, the more easily you will be able to find ways of influencing her.

You won't be able to influence your boss if you can't understand his point of view, or if you don't like him, and it shows. Bosses are human, and respond to the courtesies and thoughtfulness that other humans respond to! Find out what your boss wants and deliver it. That's the best way to influence him favourably. If your boss asks you a question, answer *that* question. Don't answer a question he *hasn't* asked without answering the question he has asked. Try to understand the question in his context. Work out what your boss needs to know so that he can persuade others. Always try to make the best of your bosses, even of the poorer ones. If they aren't good at their job it may not be entirely their fault. It may be a development job, or there may be problems with the organisational structure. Try to understand this, and provide help and support.

Your boss will be very much aware of whether you are trying to co-operate, or whether you are hostile and contemptuous. People who acquire a reputation for being contemptuous and difficult with several of their bosses won't be seen as having the maturity they need for senior jobs.

Too often we stereotype our bosses, and forget that they are people. So accustomed are managers to thinking about their subordinates, that they can find it difficult to make the switch to considering the problems of people above them. The problem is that when your boss breaks the stereotype, you will probably believe that he or she is playing politics. In fact, it could simply be that you have stereotyped him or her too rigidly in the first place.

DEALING WITH SENIOR PEOPLE

One of the keys to being able to influence senior people is developing the confidence to see yourself as having just as many rights as they have, and as deserving as much respect. Many people find it difficult to stand up to and influence senior people for two reasons. Since your boss does have some power over you, you may make the mistake of conceding special human rights to him. When you do this you deny *yourself* certain human rights, like the right to be treated with respect or to express a point of view. You increase the rights of your boss while diminishing your own rights. In reality there is no need for this. Your boss may have greater power, but not greater rights.

Secondly, people often believe that if they behave in ways that are unpopular with their boss, the boss will use or misuse his power against them. This is a distinct possibility and should be taken into account. However, it is probably the expectation of this misuse of power rather than the likelihood of it happening that prevents most people from asserting themselves with their boss. The truth is that bosses respond favourably to requests, disagreements and discussions, as long as these are put assertively, and at the appropriate time and place. Many senior people complain that the managers below them won't speak up when they disagree, and the senior person only gets to hear of the disagreement through the grapevine.

People often make a big deal out of interactions with senior people by worrying that disastrous but highly improbable consequences are sure to be forthcoming. There are usually checks and balances in any organisation that thwart the misuse of power before it occurs, or that can correct a grievance after it has occurred. *In extremis*, the right of appeal does exist. So the inner dialogue which cautions us against asserting ourselves with senior people is usually counterproductive. Those voices in the back of your mind saying 'watch it, it's dangerous to say what you think' may not be doing you a favour at all.

There are several common counterproductive beliefs concerning assertion with senior people. You need to recognise them and deal with them in your own head before you can deal effectively with your boss. Here are some examples.[6]

'Since my boss is such a well-known expert in that area, someone like me can't just question her position on that issue.'

Why is this so? What you're telling yourself is that you are not worthy enough, that you don't have the right to say that you don't understand, or don't agree. Maybe you're even saying that you don't want to appear ignorant. You are denying yourself the right to raise questions or to disagree with the other person. You are saying that your boss has certain rights and privileges (like the right not to be challenged) because of her position and you have not. You need to remind yourself that this is not the case. You have the same rights as your boss to ask questions, express opinions and raise disagreements. In fact, your boss won't respect you for denying yourself this right.

'If I state my opinion she will deny my salary increase, or find some other way of penalising me for what I think.'

Is this true? It is certainly possible. There *are* people who seek revenge when others say things they don't like. However, it doesn't occur that frequently. It certainly doesn't happen frequently enough to make you live in fear of reprisals if you state an unpopular opinion. You will be more effective if you say what you feel you need to say and take your chances with the consequences. In the unlikely event that reprisals do occur you can appeal to *her* boss.

'If my boss wants me to tackle a job in a way that I know will be ineffective, I should do it his way. Otherwise he will consider me to be unco-operative.'

Is it in your interests to take this point of view? If you do the job in an ineffective way, even if it's not your fault, you will be associated with poor results. This is possibly a bigger risk to your reputation than appearing unco-operative. 'I told you so' has no room in an influential manager's vocabulary. Your boss will not admire you for proving him to be wrong. It's your responsibility to convince him that he is wrong *before* he makes you do the job in an ineffective way. You have a right to make an informed decision on how to approach a piece of work, and to stand up for that decision. People who say, 'no, that isn't right' occasionally, are usually listened to. It's only people who are always saying 'no' who are seen as unco-operative.

EMOTIONAL ASPECTS

There will be emotional undertones to all your dealings with your boss. Even though you may be discussing a seemingly bland, technical subject, don't make the assumption that there are no emotions around. You may both be unaware of these emotions, but the 'boss-subordinate' relationship is a highly emotionally charged one. Interaction between two people is characterised by a constant struggle for power. Sometimes this is violent and clearly expressed, sometimes it is very subtle. In your relationship with your boss this will always be under the surface. Power sweeps back and forth between people, even in a single conversation. To manage your relationship with your boss you need to be aware of this. You need to avoid backing down from correctly asserting yourself because you fear the consequences of any challenge to his power. On the other hand you may need to plan your approach and discussion carefully so that you don't court rejection for your proposals by being unduly threatening to his power. To achieve this fine balance you need to put yourself into his shoes and see the world through his spectacles.

SEE THINGS FROM YOUR BOSS'S POINT OF VIEW

To be successful at influencing your boss you have to accept that there are probably profound differences in perspective between you. Middle managers suffer from more immediate pressures than their bosses. Their nightmares are filled with problems of workload, meeting deadlines and resourcing inadequacies. Their attention is very directly focused on getting the best out of the people below them and producing results for their department. The complaint from senior people is that middle managers can't grasp the larger picture, and do not accept the need to balance short-run and long-run considerations. They also see middle managers as not being helpful enough to other units in the same division.

'What you see depends on where you stand.' Senior managers have to take a more strategic long-term point of view. The business would soon flounder if they only thought about immediate pressures to produce for current demand. They also have to worry about the integration and resourcing of all the departments under their control. If you try to influence your boss with arguments that only focus on the needs and plans of *your* part of the organisation, you may fail because you aren't seeing the whole picture, like he has to.

A typical scenario

Fred, the manager of the drawing office, tries to persuade his boss Elaine to award especially large pay increases on merit to two particularly good draughtsmen. These two will probably leave if they don't get a good pay increase, because they are being courted by a large competitor who is offering higher salaries. Elaine, his boss, is sympathetic, but has a limited budget, and has to consider similar pleas from two of the three other units in her division. She can only offer a third of what Fred is asking for. If Fred got his way all the available merit pay would go to his unit and there would be none left over for the others. Fred chooses a typically ineffective influence strategy. He is desperate to keep his draughtsmen because of their specialist experience. He fights nearly to the finish with Elaine over this issue. In the end she refuses to give any more, and curtly ends the debate, fed up with Fred's inability to see her problems or to consider another solution. Fred loses ungraciously. He goes back to his draughtsmen and accuses Elaine of being stingy. This reinforces the negative attitude the draughtsmen have towards top management and in six months they have both left. They didn't leave just because of the money, but because they didn't like the atmosphere within the company. Without his two top draughtsmen, Fred's unit cannot deliver and his reputation takes a knock.

What would have been a more effective approach?

Fred would have stood a better chance of success if he had prepared himself for his meeting with Elaine by putting himself in her shoes. It is obvious that he cannot get all the money he wants, but he may have got more had he argued from Elaine's perspective rather than his. He could have said something like:

'I can see your problem. You only have £3,000 to give in merit pay, and your unit managers are asking for merit increases for six staff. So you are thinking of giving each person £500. Obviously, my request of £1,500 for each of my draughtsmen is unrealistic, but let's look at all of the deserving cases and see whether a different division of the spoils wouldn't be more in the company's interests.'

Fred and Elaine could then review the opportunities for each of the deserving individuals to change jobs, the cost to the company of losing them, the problems and costs of replacing them, and the difficulties of training their replacements. Chances are that this analysis will show that Fred's draughtsmen, with their specialist skills and experience, are more difficult and expensive to replace than the other people in the equation. Together, he and Elaine could agree a compromise which gives them more money, but still leaves some for the other contenders. If Fred's draughtsmen are not more costly or difficult to replace then he doesn't have a case for getting them more than £500 each. If this is so he should give in gracefully, make his position clear, and seek other rewards in other ways and at other times for his draughtsmen. He should go back and explain the whole picture to these people, and make it clear that they are very much appreciated and that he is doing his best for them, but that there are understandable constraints.

OVERCOMING BARRIERS TO UPWARD INFLUENCE

Weed out the minor complaints

Senior people complain that middle managers have difficulty in distinguishing between major and minor issues. They talk to their bosses about too many things. You need to learn to weed out the minor complaints, the irrelevant detail and the matters you can deal with yourself. There is nothing to be gained, except for a reputation as a trouble-maker, by asserting yourself with your boss about every little detail of your job or of his behaviour that doesn't meet completely with your approval. There is also no point in raising too many matters or asking for too many decisions. The effect of such overcommunication is to make it less likely that he will pay attention to you when you have an important concern to voice.

Keep an open mind

Another complaint from senior people is that those below them anticipate their reaction to a request, instead of putting the case and keeping
an open mind about the answer. If at the start of an attempt to influence
your boss you assume that the answer is going to be 'no', then your
efforts are doomed to failure. Too many people simply talk themselves
out of possible success where they make such negative assumptions.
Enthusiasm and optimism are influential emotions and it's a shame to
weaken your case by discarding them.

Give the full truth

Often, managers don't give the full truth about the possible disadvantages of their proposals. They simply hope for the best as far as the
possible drawbacks are concerned, instead of confronting all available
information openly and honestly. This is no way to build up your
influence with your boss. He won't trust you in the future, if you don't
give warnings about things that might go wrong with your schemes.

Don't surprise your boss

All the managers that I interviewed had this to say about bosses – they
don't like surprises, and they don't like half-baked ideas. When you
have to influence your boss plan ahead and try to work out your strategy.
You won't be successful all the time, but you are not just going for short-
term gains. You also have a longer term aim of favourably influencing
your boss's view of you as a competent, trustworthy person, with
potential for higher things.

It is important to lobby. You can't just confront your boss, either
alone or at a meeting, with a completely new proposal and hope to get
instant support. If you try to influence this way you will find it very time-
consuming, and the chances are that you will fail. If your boss is inclined
to say no initially, give her room to manoeuvre, and a way to change her
mind yet retain credibility. Find a way of making it easy for your boss to
make the decision.

Remember that one decision will have an impact on others. You have
to see the wider picture and work through all the potential problems.
This takes time and thought, and is the reason why sudden surprise
proposals will often get a 'no'. When you are flexible about changing

your mind, you stand a better chance of influencing your boss. Too many people fail because they are inflexible and intransigent.

Influencing our boss is not only about being political and empathising. It is also about having sound proposals that are well thought through. If you frequently pester your boss with unworkable ideas you will soon train him to ignore you. Prepare well. Don't go in to your boss with a half-baked idea. Make sure your proposal is well thought out and that you have a good plan for its implementation. Then you will get the bulk of your proposal through. On more politically sensitive issues talk about the issue with lots of people. Speak to people who have the ear of your boss, and eventually it gets back to him. Sometimes your boss will then come and speak to you about the issue and you can sort it out together.

Here is an example of another manager's attempt to influence his boss (the chairman in this case) on a politically sensitive subject.

When I had been a director for a short while I realised that there was a problem person on the board. We were going through times of change and he was not prepared to change fast enough. I thought about it, and realised that the board couldn't work as a cohesive unit with him there, and we needed to pull together in difficult times. Of the ten people on the board I knew that five others felt the same, and possibly one or two others, although I couldn't rely on it. As a new board member I was very much feeling my way about my influence with the chairman. I decided I had to talk to the chairman (my boss) about it, as all of our futures were at stake. I took him out for a drink and told him how I saw the problem. I said that we would all be in trouble if we didn't get results, and that several of us saw this problem person as holding us back. I had to say to my boss that if he didn't deal with this problem, then we would be at risk. I was listened to sympathetically.

This manager was wise enough not to raise such a sensitive issue in public, at a board meeting, or in front of a number of other managers. Delicate problems need delicate treatment. If he hadn't built up an informal relationship with his boss he would have been unable to deal with this problem in this way. Your boss won't thank you for raising difficult problems out of the blue in meetings. He would prefer to be given time to think through his response beforehand.

If you disagree with your boss in public then you're heading into danger. If you can't agree with him, and in your judgement the issue is worth it (from a company point of view), then arrange through your boss to take the matter to his boss, but be sure of your ground and be prepared to concede. There isn't a boss in the world who will not see you as disloyal if you disagree with or criticise him in public. Once you are seen as disloyal then you have lost your influence.

When you go to your boss with a proposal give him:

- time to think about it;
- the reassurance that at least some of your colleagues agree with it;
- a mature, non-pressurising approach from you.

Keith Manning keeps these things in mind when he wants to influence his boss.

First of all, think through who else in the company would be affected by your project and make sure you talk to them first. Never go to your boss with a project you've not talked through with other people. People don't like surprises. I know that when I am making a decision I talk to two or three subordinates and then think about it. When I go to my boss with a proposal he is going to wonder what everyone else will be thinking about it. If I've catered for this by finding out first then it makes it easier. If some of my colleagues disagree with my proposal, I talk it through with my boss, and then again with the colleagues separately. Sometimes it isn't possible or appropriate to take it any further, and you've got to develop the judgement to recognise when it's not on.

GET TO KNOW YOUR BOSS

Too many managers fail to influence their bosses because they perceive them inaccurately. You have to learn how your boss thinks. You must be aware of your boss's:

- pressures;
- priorities;
- emotions;
- style; and
- preferences.

Mike Dearden says:

You have got to know the person you're dealing with. You must know his preferences, his priorities and his foibles. The last two chief executives in Castrol have been very different indeed. They emphasise different priorities, and have very different personal styles and approaches to life.

The first was a non-graduate who rose through the ranks to the top. He was a company man, very loyal, with a lot of experience in the UK. He surrounded himself with practical, experienced people. He was a bottom-line person, and very interested in the detail. He would reject a proposal if the detail was wrong. He was replaced by a chief executive who is very bright and intellectual. He has a flexible, open approach and he doesn't concern himself so much with detail.

The first chief executive would feel the need to accept a proposal if the detail was right, even if the concept was flawed. The current chief executive accepts a good concept, even if the detail is not perfect. I also had to know who they turned to for advice. The first chief executive turned to his experienced line managers for advice, he avoided professionals whom he saw as 'woolly theoreticians'. The current chief executive is just the opposite. He surrounds himself with professional advisers rather than line managers.

My approach to influencing my boss had to change dramatically. In the past I used to worry about getting the detail right. Now I work hard to put forward good concepts, and to present them persuasively. I make sure that the chief executive's advisers agree with the concepts before I see him with my proposals. I avoid putting up proposals that will get shot down. It's a waste of time and not good for my reputation. I pre-sell to someone influential (like the finance director) and then ask the chief executive to discuss my proposal with him. This pre-selling enhances the quality of my proposals, because I can learn from the people I pre-sell to. They often know something I don't know, or have better ideas.

If you get to know your boss, and spend time talking to him, you will find it easier to get his attention when you need to discuss something important. But you must avoid making a bad impression by producing ideas which have not been carefully thought through. You may find it useful to take it in two stages. First of all you need to attract his attention so say something like, 'I think we have a problem here and we need to discuss the solution.' Then when your boss says, 'What do you think we should do?', instead of giving him a half-baked proposal, set up a meeting in the near future which gives you time to prepare yourself, by discussing with colleagues and thinking it all through. You can easily say, 'I think this problem needs more than a quick discussion. Can we fix a meeting in a few days time when we can explore it more thoroughly?'

Keith Manning agrees with this point:

> Get to know your boss well. Communicate regularly with him, both formally and informally. This can be difficult because of time pressures. When unexpected opportunities arise to talk to your boss resist the temptation to go off at half cock and sell him ideas that you haven't thought through properly. I can get to see my boss either very early or very late. When I want to say something significant I establish that we need to have a serious discussion, then set up a time and get prepared.

SAYING 'NO' TO YOUR BOSS

To be influential with your boss you have got to learn to say 'no' to him when it's appropriate. Your boss will never come to rely on you and trust you if you don't alert him to danger, warn against wrong decisions and stand up for what you know to be right. Saying 'no' is perfectly valid. Make sure that your joint understanding of the interests of the company is clear. The reasons for saying 'no' are usually about the interests of the company.

You have to prepare the ground for saying 'no'. Your boss must see you as loyal first before she will take 'no' from you. This means that you will need to have given a lot of willing 'yeses' in the recent past. People who have proved themselves loyal subordinates are allowed the greatest amount of free speech and criticism. The subordinate who cannot stop objecting, and who doesn't respond quickly and unstintingly to requests, is the one who loses influence upwards. You also demonstrate loyalty and gain influence by keeping the boss informed of any problems that may cause embarrassment or disappointment.

When to play it safe

There are times when it is dangerous to say 'no', and when compliance is in your best interests.[4]

- When your boss is insecure or despotic.
- When the situation is highly political and threats are about. When loyalty is the main quality required of you.

- When there is an environment of zero trust. (Although you should try to move if this goes on too long.)
- When you are new and unknowing. When, for example, you have a new job, a new boss or your work is changing direction. In these cases you should lie low and work hard to build trust for at least six months.
- When survival is at stake (unless you're sinking because you haven't stood up for your ideas in the past).
- Following periods of risk or expansion.
- When it is difficult for your performance to be evaluated because of the nature of your work. (There are no obvious results.) When absence of friction is more important than performance.

INFLUENCING AN AUTOCRATIC BOSS

Here are some rules for persuading an autocratic boss on a big decision. Prepare the ground carefully. Don't spring your proposal on your boss. Keep up your contact and dialogue beforehand. Avoid presenting both the problem and the solution at the same time – it will feel too pressurising to her. Your strategy should be to present the problem in stages, and in such a way that no solution will be immediately obvious. This way your boss will not commit herself to an inadequate solution before you have had a chance to make your full case. Once an autocratic person has committed herself it is almost impossible to get them to change their mind.[4]

DEALING WITH A BAD BOSS

There is no guarantee that you will always have a boss who is reasonable and competent. Bosses come in all shapes and sizes and you have to learn to deal with them even when they are incompetent, cowardly, uncommunicative, interfering or dishonest.

Here is some advice on how to deal with insecure bosses who need to be kept informed over every detail, and who interfere and hold you back. Try to agree a set of rules and blow the whistle when your boss breaks them. You do need to have it out with your boss if he keeps interfering, otherwise he will keep on doing it and you'll feel resentful. The worst thing you can do is to blame your boss in front of other people.

If you have built up a relationship with your boss then you will be able to raise a delicate problem like his interference. If, however, this interference puts your teeth on edge, and you have not established rapport, then it will be difficult to criticise your boss, even in private.

Sometimes you may get lumbered with a boss you really dislike or disapprove of. Then it is difficult to manage your relationship well. To establish a good relationship with your boss you've got to communicate with him, and if you disapprove of him, this can be very hard. Your boss will know that you disapprove of him and will see you as a threat. You will find yourself treading on thin ice and will have to find ways of protecting yourself. Martin Smith once found himself in this position.

> My relationship with this manager was not good. I don't like people who advance their careers through manipulation and behind-the-scenes dealings, and I felt he had some of those characteristics. As I didn't like him I couldn't manage the relationship the normal way, through communication. So I had to find other seniors with whom to communicate. I also had to make sure that I produced a consistently high performance.

Mike Dearden has also had to deal with a boss he dislikes.

> I was once bulldozed into taking on a job by a particularly unpleasant man. To persuade me to agree he said – you must know that you are being considered for other things. If you don't take this job then your judgement will be considered lacking and you won't get your hoped-for career moves. I took the job, but did not like this boss at all. He tried to spike me with black influence. We had a completely different approach to work and he saw me as a threat. He wasn't prepared to give me the freedom I had been promised. I suffered this for two months and then started making lateral alliances to make my views known. My boss and I had a running battle for twelve months. In the end I managed to escape from working for him through a combination of methods:
>
> - I sent copies of memos to the right people;
> - I insisted on getting my views across on my appraisal documents;
> - I used the formal system in every way I could;
> - I used my informal networks.

The worst thing you can do for your career is to spend too long working for an incompetent boss. If your department has a bad reputation because of your boss's mismanagement, then you will be tarred with the same brush. Do whatever you can to move to another department, or even get the company to get rid of him if you think you can swing it.

Getting rid of an incompetent boss

Here is some advice on how to get rid of a poor boss. If your boss is useless, plan accordingly, but don't let him see you as a threat early on. Situations will arise where his incompetence is demonstrated. If you're credible at the time you can go over your boss's head and say something has got to be done. The power-seeker will do that in a sophisticated way, by documenting it properly, giving times, dates and details. People underestimate how easy it is to remove an incompetent boss. If you boss is not incompetent but you don't like him, then live with him, or move. It is not easy to change people. Come to a truce. Have your battles, then agree a demarcation line.

DON'T HITCH YOUR WAGGON TOO CLOSELY TO YOUR BOSS'S STAR

There is also a danger in getting so close to your boss that you are totally dependent on his success. John Mills has this story to tell.

> I had a great boss once. He and I thought similarly and we got a lot done together. He died suddenly, and this left me with a real problem. Many of our joint projects had been seen as UDIish by the parent company. As soon as my boss died the 'hawks' from the parent company got in and enlarged their empires at my expense. I was caught. I did not have friends and allies in the parent company. I did not stay for long afterwards.

John was caught because he had developed his relationship with only one senior person, and had no other allies to protect him when that person went. A good relationship with your boss is invaluable, but you also need other friends.

In summary:

- get to know your boss and learn to see things from his point of view;
- give your boss loyalty and support, so that he comes to trust you and listens to you;
- remember that not all bosses thrive on yeses;

- say 'no' when it's right to do so, but back it up with sound reasoning;
- when you need to influence your boss plan your case and your strategy based on your knowledge of his pressures and preferences.

CHAPTER 7

INFLUENCING AT MEETINGS

If you want to be more powerful, you need to shine at meetings. Use meetings as an opportunity to get known, extend your influence, make contacts outside of your department or level and attract sponsors. You can also use meetings as a way of attracting junior people in other departments to come and work for you.

This can sound like hard advice to follow if you generally find meetings to be boring, frustrating, overpowering or unproductive. Sometimes meetings can be all of these things. It's hardly surprising that people who lack the skills to influence meetings hate being there, and can hardly wait for them to be over so that they can get back to work. Such people can easily come to see meetings as a waste of time, and not worth putting any effort into. If you take that point of view, however, you will limit your power, because meetings are often the most politically significant events at work.

The way to see meetings is as an opportunity to sell yourself to other people in the organisation. Also, if you have meetings with people from outside the company, they can provide you with opportunities to make wider contacts in your field. You never know when you might find these contacts useful in finding a job in the future. Impressive behaviour at meetings is much more likely to get you noticed and help you to get on, than what you do back at your own desk. Of course if you get consistently poor results, then being a whiz at meetings won't save you in the end. But getting good results, combined with being a sour-faced boor at meetings, is not a formula for success. Meetings are public arenas, so learn to respect them as such and develop the skills you need to be influential there. Remember also being a good leader means being a good advocate for your group. It will often be at meetings that you will have to present your case to get approval for your group's projects, get the resources they need and negotiate co-operation. So if you let yourself down, you will also be letting your subordinates down.

MAKE ALLIES NOT ENEMIES

The influential manager uses meetings as an opportunity to make allies, not enemies. It's all too easy to make enemies by the way you behave in meetings. Managers often go to meetings so intent on fighting for what they want that they accidentally offend their colleagues. Interrupting, ignoring people, disagreeing with them curtly and putting them down in public, are all ways of making enemies. You shouldn't let poor ideas get accepted just for the sake of politeness, but there are ways of influencing others at meetings which are positive and will leave you with more friends than enemies.

Influencing meetings is a much more complicated activity than influencing individuals. You do have to think about getting in, getting action and getting out, but you also have to understand group dynamics. How the individuals in the group respond to you will depend on your ability to speak convincingly, but it will also depend on the politics in the group. A group does not behave just like a straightforward multiple of all the individuals within it. Groups seem to have a dynamic of their own and it is worth being alert to this, because it will affect your chances of influencing and will determine the best strategy to use. If you become aware of what is going on in the group, you stand a better chance of being able to influence that group, even if you are not in the chair.

LEARN ABOUT GROUP 'PROCESS'

To understand what is happening at a meeting you have to learn to distinguish between 'content' and 'process'. *Content* deals with the subject matter or task that the group is working on. If the meeting is making a decision on the reallocation of car parking spaces, then that is the content of that meeting, or of that part of the agenda. In most meetings, the focus of attention of all members is on the content.

Process is all about what is happening between, and to, group members while the group is working. Process is how the group goes about making its decisions or solving its problems. It deals with such factors as morale, feelings, atmosphere, influence, participation, leadership, conflict and co-operation. Process is very important to the quality of the decisions made at a meeting. Even if the people at the meeting have the necessary knowledge and experience, they can still come up with a bad decision if the process at the meeting is poor. Yet very little attention is paid to process by most managers. Many of them have never heard of the concept. If you develop a sensitivity to group process it will enable you to understand what is happening in the group, and it will give you the information you need to help the group to deal with problems, and to steer them towards high-quality decisions. You can do this even if you are not in the chair, although the chairperson does have a lot of power to influence group process. Understanding about group process, and developing the skills to influence it, can make you very influential in your meetings.

There are two types of group process, 'task' and 'maintenance'. Both these concepts are discussed below.

Task process

This is any behaviour which is trying to get the group to accomplish its task. In the meeting on reallocating car parking spaces, for example, any intervention which directly helps the group to make a decision on that subject comes under the heading of task process. Here are some examples:

- *Initiating*. This means proposing goals or tasks: defining the problem; identifying obstacles; and suggesting an idea or procedure for solving a problem. Under this heading you can influence the group enormously by suggesting a suitable structure for collecting information and making the decision systematically. You can propose the stages the group need to go through to make a good decision.

- *Seeking information*. The whole advantage of meetings is that several heads are better than one. I've seen so many bad chairpersons plough their way through a meeting without tapping into a fraction of the knowledge and expertise of the people sitting around the table. If you actively seek ways of using this experience you will undoubtedly raise the quality of the final decision. You can ask for facts, seek background information, or look for ideas and suggestions.

- *Giving information.* Often you will be one of the people sitting there with relevant information, so make sure you give it and give it at the time that it is needed. Too often I see people allow the group to come to a firm decision, and then try to throw a spanner in the works at the eleventh hour by producing new information which opens up a question on the decision. Not only might this make you unpopular, but the chances are you will be ignored. It's a known fact of group dynamics that once the meeting feels it has made a decision it is very reluctant to rethink it. So make sure you give your information at the early stages of decision-making when it can contribute. You can offer facts or background information, state beliefs and opinions, or give suggestions or ideas.

- *Clarifying.* You will be seen as helpful and influential if you spend some time clarifying. You can interpret ideas or suggestions, clear up confusions, define terms or indicate alternatives and issues. So much time can be wasted in a meeting by people talking at cross-purposes, or arguing from different assumptions. Anything you can do to reduce this sort of confusion will speed up the group's work.

- *Summarising.* Meetings can be very confusing. Individuals some- times get lost, or forget points that have been previously aired or agreed. There is too much going on for everyone to keep everything in their heads. It helps for someone, at intervals, to summarise. This will include pulling together related ideas, restating suggestions after the group has discussed them, or offering a decision or conclusion for the meeting to accept or reject.

Other task process behaviours include:

- helping the group to plan how it is going to tackle a task;
- timing and checking progress;
- making lists.

Maintenance process

This is any sort of behaviour which helps the group to remain in good working order. Maintenance is about creating a good atmosphere for working on the task and about creating good working relationships within the group. Here are some examples of maintenance.

107

- *Harmonising*. It is inevitable that there will be some disagreement at most meetings. In fact it is healthy for people to discuss differences. Some conflict can lead to better and more creative solutions. What you don't want is the emotional temperature to get so high that the conflicts cause only heat and no light. When you see that conflict is getting unproductive then it is time to harmonise. Just try to help people to reconcile disagreements. Reduce tensions and get people to explore differences rather than get into entrenched positions.

- *Gatekeeping*. Getting air space in a meeting can be a problem, especially for less experienced or shy people. Competition to get a word in can be quite intense. The people who don't get heard, or who withdraw from the fray, may be those who have something valuable to contribute. Meetings entirely dominated by confident people and wind-bags don't usually get all the information and ideas they need for making good decisions. You can play a very influential role by doing some gatekeeping. Help to keep the communication channels open. Make sure that everyone participates and that ideas are heard and discussed. If people are interrupted or ignored when they say something valuable, invite them to restate their point. Without your support they may not try again. Ask the quiet people for their views. Less experienced people will often be glad to speak if they are invited to do so, but may not have the courage, timing or skill to break into the flow on their own.

- *Encouraging*. Be friendly and supportive to other people at the meeting. Indicate by brief remarks or just nods and smiles when you agree with another person's contribution. Pay attention to the other people at the meeting and listen to what they are saying. If you go to a meeting with the attitude that people other than you may have something positive to contribute, then you will be a better listener. The others will find you more encouraging. This may seem like such a simple thing, but it does influence the meeting. If only one or two people are encouraging it alters the atmosphere in the room dramatically. People feel less tense, more inclined to say what they think, and as a result often come up with more creative solutions.

- *Developing ideas*. This is probably the most influential thing you can do in a meeting. When someone else suggests a good idea, support it, and develop it further, adding any ideas you may have which will strengthen it. An example could go something like this:

'Why don't we do some customer-care training to improve service at our outlets?'

'What a good idea. We could also change our appraisal system so that people are appraised on the way they handle the customer. This would reinforce the training.

By supporting and developing this initial suggestion, you make sure that it gets aired and discussed by the meeting. If two people (or more) are behind a proposal it increases the chances that the proposal will be accepted. This is why people lobby before meetings of course. It is another law of group dynamics that people are more inclined to take a proposal seriously if they think that several group members are behind it.

EMOTIONAL PROBLEMS IN GROUPS

The reason why meetings are often complicated affairs which need good group process is that there are always emotional problems lurking beneath the surface. There are so many forces which are active in groups that disturb work and form an emotional undercurrent in the stream of group life. These undercurrents produce behaviour which can make it difficult for the meeting to function properly. People usually try to ignore these issues or wish them away. The influential group member will recognise such issues and then encourage the group to discuss and deal with issues which are blocking group progress. Often the culture in the meeting is such that feelings and problems cannot be openly discussed. Then, at the very least, the person who is alert to these problems has an advantage. He or she can use their understanding to prevent themselves being made impotent by the undercurrents, and also use their group process skills to alleviate the problems.

Here are some examples of emotional issues.

Identity

People often feel uncertain about their identity in meetings. They struggle with questions like:

- Where do I fit into this meeting?
- What can I say, and what shouldn't I say?
- What kind of behaviour is acceptable here?

Goals and needs

Usually, people go to meetings with either open or hidden agendas of their own. They ask themselves questions like:

- What do I want from this meeting?
- Can the group goals be made consistent with my goals?
- What do I have to offer this meeting?

Power

Often, issues of power and influence are the most disrupting undercurrents. There are questions such as:

- Who will control what we do?
- Will people listen to my proposals and take me seriously?
- Do I have enough allies to help me win my battles?
- How much power and influence do I have?

Intimacy

There will also be issues of intimacy and trust, raising questions like:

- How personal is the discussion likely to get?
- How much can we trust each other?

In a meeting where there is no one with the power, skill or awareness to help the group to deal with these issues, problems will certainly arise. Here are some examples of the destructive behaviour which emotional issues can produce.

Counterdependency

People who feel frustrated or resentful may oppose or resist anyone in the meeting who represents authority. In most cases this will not be done openly, but even in a subtle form it can be quite damaging. People feeling like this will simply argue against proposals, giving reasons which don't reflect what they are actually feeling. Because they don't give the real reason, they are impossible to win over and this can block the meeting's ability to make decisions.

Dominating

It is very common in meetings that one or two strong people assert their personal dominance, and attempt to get their own way, regardless of others. This can be crudely and aggressively done. But sometimes a manager can dominate a meeting simply by talking too much, interrupting or ignoring other people and listening only so that he or she can argue back. Even a pleasant, genial person who talks too much can be experienced as dominating. It's a way of negatively exerting influence and power. It may work for the person doing it, but it causes problems for the meeting and can be counterproductive.

Withdrawing

Some people simply withdraw in the face of failure to meet their goals and exert influence. They don't leave the room, but you can see by their glassy stare and slumped posture that they are not with you any more. They are trying to remove the source of uncomfortable feelings by not contributing for long periods and psychologically leaving the group.

Pairing up

Sometimes two (or more) people will form a kind of emotional subgroup where they protect and support one another. It is a defensive action against the rest of the group and doesn't help objectivity!

DEVELOP PROCESS SKILLS TO INFLUENCE MEETINGS

The big question is what behaviour favourably influences a meeting and helps it to accomplish its task? We need to learn what behaviour makes an individual significant to that meeting, and able to control (at least to some extent) the direction of the meeting and the final result.

First of all you can become significant to the meeting by being alert to what is going on and by making contributions at the process level, as well as at the content level. This includes both task and maintenance process. All the behaviours described under those headings will be useful at different times.

Both Tom Nell and Keith Manning are aware that process skills can help them to favourably influence meetings. Tom Nell says:

> One way of influencing a meeting is by being good at process. Take notes as a way of contributing and use the notes to help you summarise and clarify. Volunteer to be the scribe, if it is acceptable in your company culture. Draw out the quieter members of the meeting. Ask open questions and help formulate proposals and policies. It all helps to make you influential.

Keith Manning advises:

> Timing in meetings is very important. A little reinforcing comment helps when someone else makes a proposal that you are in sympathy with. Be alert to what is happening in the meeting. Use your awareness of what is going on to get things agreed quickly. Knowing what is going on really matters.

Developing process skills puts you in a position where you can be seen to be a constructive positive influence on the group. It is stage one in the battle to make allies rather than enemies. It not only leads towards a better result, but it also gives you a personal advantage, in a way which does not create enemies. It doesn't detract from your power to be sensitive to other people's problems, in fact it adds to it.

'Oh, I can't let issues like emotional problems distract me,' you may say. 'I haven't got the time to worry about things like that. I just want to go in there and get my proposals through.' The danger with that point of view is that you are ignoring the obstacles to your success, and you may end up wasting time or failing. It is good meeting strategy to understand about process; it enhances your chances of success. If you simply focus on your proposals and arguments, and fail to listen to other people, you will generate resistance. You will also probably fail to spot opportunities to build alliances with other people who could have helped you to argue for your case. If you have sound proposals, but frequently fail to get them accepted in meetings, try to stand back and work out why. It may be that you are trying to dominate the meeting and people are resisting you because of that, regardless of the strength of your proposals. Next time try to do some clarifying and encouraging. Invite other people to express their ideas. Support and develop any proposals from others that you think may have promise. You'll be surprised at how much more inclined people will be to listen to your proposals if you behave like that.

Don't threaten

Most of the managers I interviewed were aware of the emotional problems that can block your influence in a meeting. Their advice is to avoid threatening or diminishing people in public in meetings, because it just doesn't get you anywhere.

Try not to force other people into entrenched positions. If you confront powerful people directly they will take a strong position in defence, and then they can't climb down – so you lose. Try to back off and look for another way around the wall. Don't go into attack. Ask questions about a proposal you don't like, but don't attack the proposer. Open up the debate by asking a question about whatever aspect you're concerned about. Most key decisions are made before the meeting starts, so do some lobbying. Lobbying is so much more productive than trying to batter your head against a brick wall in the meeting.

Presenting bad news

Rosie Harris says:

> Don't go in like a bull in a china shop. I've been involved, as the financial person, in a project since 1987. When I first started attending the meetings I was rather wary. The others were very powerful. I was there to give advice and to be the devil's advocate. The chairman didn't like to hear bad news, but to be realistic I *had* to give bad news sometimes, and cause frustration. I was the only woman in the group. I formed a close contact with one other person in the group and I bounced ideas off him before throwing them into the group. I learnt to think before speaking, rather than wade in regardless. I learnt to say things like, 'What are our objectives in doing this?' or 'I don't understand why we're doing this.' Of course, as financial adviser, I was often having to say negative things. But I said them in a quiet, down-to-earth way and wasn't aggressive about it. Now I feel more self-confident and know all the other players better.

People will be much more inclined to consider your proposals and even your criticisms if you put them in a positive way. You will be seen in a better light if you consistently try to seek solutions, rather than complain a lot or put people down for what you consider to be poor decisions. Try to make positive rather than negative remarks. You always have a choice. Here are some positive ways of reconstructing negative remarks.

'I think your proposal is out of court because it would be far too expensive.'
Instead, try saying: 'That's a possibility we could consider. In its present form the proposal is too costly, but we could find ways of modifying it to make it more feasible. Or perhaps we could come up with a less expensive alternative which would achieve the same aim.'

'No, I'm sorry, we can't accept your proposal to collaborate. I think you're in fantasy land if you imagine your organisation is ready to work with ours.' (This was said to a visiting company director from the Soviet Union.)
Instead, the manager in question could have said: 'I am grateful for your offer to collaborate. I don't think the time is right, but I hope that we may be able to work together in the future. I should be honoured by such an association.'

In both cases, the first, negative response was destined to make enemies, and it did!

Remember that you can also be negative with your body language. If you fail to look at people, look bored, cross or ferocious (many people actually look ferocious in meetings) and slouch in your chair, you will give negative messages that will be clearly read by everybody. Often, people withdraw when they are unhappy with events, and this is also seen as negative behaviour. If you want to influence the meeting you need to look alert but relaxed, sit up straight and maintain eye contact.

Many people don't realise the value of non-verbal communication. Use your body position, lean forward, and show enthusiasm and animation. Sit next to someone whose support you want. It diffuses potential conflict. Even in a time of real conflict in a meeting a smile or a wink can soften things a lot. Non-verbal communication is very powerful; use it to reduce any threat you may appear to pose.

Handling criticism

My advise about criticising other people in a meeting is simple. Don't do it. It only causes problems and never achieves what you want it to. If the person on the receiving end is senior, you will make a personal enemy, and if he is junior it will be traumatic for him. In either case public criticism will engender defensive behaviour. The person criticised will put his or her energy into giving explanations and excuses, or into counterattacking, rather than into putting the situation right. I'm not saying don't criticise; I'm just saying don't do it in public, in a meeting. Take the individual aside, either before or after the meeting and give the criticism, and discuss it in private. This way you're much more likely to get a constructive response.

If *you* are criticised in a meeting, try to handle it with as much dignity as possible. Even if you are being unfairly treated, if you react to it badly you will unfortunately create a bad impression. In Chapter 9 there is detailed advice on how to handle criticism, both the just and the unjust kind. This advice is particularly relevant to meetings.

Create light rather than heat

It's common for people who feel strongly about their proposals to spoil their chances by overselling and being too intense.

To influence a meeting you need perspective, not just information. What doesn't influence a meeting is someone who goes overboard on an idea. They may do that because they can't see the wider issues. But if you don't present a balanced argument you stand less chance of succeeding. Lobby beforehand and make sure you know where everyone stands. This makes you more persuasive.

Timing is also very important. The first hour of a meeting is often taken up with unproductive positioning. Try just to listen or not say much for the first hour. People will then invite you to speak because they feel the weight of your silence. Make your proposal in the second hour, not the first. Choose your moment. If you're alert then you'll see when the time is ripe. Of course, you can only do this when you're clear about what you want.

Research into the conduct of meetings shows that the people who jump in and make the first proposals are not the people whose proposals are accepted. Those who listen, ask questions, analyse and then come up with considered proposals later on in the meeting without overselling are more likely to be successful.

Brush up on your presentation skills

If you want to create light, rather than heat, it helps if you speak well.

Keep your remarks brief and to the point, and use simple, informal language. There is nothing more off-putting than a long-winded speaker. Always go for simple, familiar words. Your spoken language is very important because it gives messages about you, just like your body language. If you are long-winded and formal you will be seen as pompous. If you are hesitant, too quietly spoken and inarticulate you will lack credibility. If you use a lot of clichés and 'filler words' you will give the impression that you don't really know what you are talking about. 'Filler' words are words and phrases that add nothing to your meaning, indeed they can obscure it. Here are some examples:

you know
at this moment in time
situation (the interview situation)
scenario (the meeting scenario)
um
basically
in due course.

We often use these trivial words and phrases to buy ourselves time to think. The more pressurised we are, the more we use them. It is a bad habit. It is far better to pause when you need to think, rather than confuse the listener and lower the impact of what you have to say with these clichés.

You should also avoid complex phrases, jargon and unfamiliar words. Poor performance when you are speaking at a meeting reduces your influence. Here are some examples of long-winded ways of saying things:

- *All properties are located within reasonable access of the motorway system.*
- *The following points are all noteworthy in respect of the region's economic success.*
- *The collapse of the oil price has necessitated a reduction in public spending and has produced a slower growth rate than has been experienced in the past.*

If you use shorter sentences and more familiar words instead your meaning is clearer and you will be easier to listen to. Try the following instead.

- All properties are close to the motorway.
- The region's economic success is due to . . .

- Both public spending and growth are down since the collapse of the oil price.

Speaking clearly and simply does make you more powerful, but it isn't easy to do at a meeting. When you are flustered and confused, pressurised to speak quickly and to defend your ideas from attack, often from very articulate people, it's easy to get it wrong. Preparation and practice will help you to improve. You can only be clear in your speech if you are clear in your mind about what you want to say. Planning your points beforehand will help you to achieve this.

If you feel you need it, try to get your company to send you on a presentation skills course. This will teach you to how to order your thoughts under pressure, and will improve your confidence. Christina Stuart's book *Effective Speaking* (Pan 1988) is also worth a read.

Watch where you sit

If you sit in a good position at a meeting this can make it easier for you to influence the discussion. The best place is opposite the chairperson, and the second best place is in the middle of either of the side rows. In these positions most people can see you and you can easily signal that you want to speak. It can be a good idea to sit directly opposite your greatest ally, because it is useful to have eye contact with him or her.

Mike Dearden has this experience to relate:

> I found myself for a year sitting on the wrong side of the chairman at board meetings. I was forever having to lean forward to catch his eye. At the first meeting of the new management board after a reorganisation I came in early and switched my name card with the card belonging to a new board member. The new board member had been placed opposite the chairman, so by switching with him I got a good seat, and have stayed in that position since then. Now that I sit opposite the chairman it makes a big difference.

PREPARATION

If every time you speak at a meeting your remarks are short, simple, clear and relevant, people will soon learn that you are worth listening to. Fluent, self-confident speakers are always more influential. However the only way you are going to achieve this is through preparation.

Tom Nell advises:

> It helps if you know in advance what the issues are. Find out what others think about what's on the agenda, and if there are hidden agendas. Be well prepared. Know what you're there to contribute, and contribute that. I ask my team to do some work on the various angles and to update and brief me before I go to meetings.

Background and homework are useful. You need to find out *beforehand* how people view your proposals. Find out their grounds for opposition. Don't try to take on your opponents single-handed. Use your peer supporters to exert pressure. Work out what *you* want from the meeting. Meetings (especially general discussion ones) are less time-wasting if you are clear what you want out of them.

Pre-plan to whom you want to say what. Don't just rely on the intellectual power of your argument. Decisions in meetings aren't just based on intellectual arguments, they are also based on who has the influence and power. You need to get the right people on your side if you hope to win through. This can involve you in a lot of homework beforehand, but it is worth it if it means you are successful in the end.

Rosie Harris also speaks about the value of preparation:

> I used not to think out what I wanted from a meeting. Now I prepare carefully. I make sure that I know the other people attending the meeting, and what stance they are going to take. I do background work with them beforehand. If you let pressure of work stop you from preparing, the danger is that you get steamrollered into doing things you shouldn't do, simply because you haven't thought through the implications.

Gather all the information and allies you need to get your proposals accepted. It is no good suggesting a new project or direction if you haven't done the costings, and haven't found out how it would affect other interested parties. Try to anticipate the questions and go in prepared with all the facts and figures you are likely to need to be persuasive. If you have a lot of detail and figures to present, prepare charts and other visual aids. Make sure that everything you show the others looks professional.

Preparation will do a lot to make you look credible and competent. Don't fail to influence because you give the wrong impression by being unprepared. Preparation doesn't only help you to work out a more convincing case, it helps you to feel more self-confident and this in turn will help you to be more fluent and clear.

CHAIRING MEETINGS

If you are in the chair, you have an even greater opportunity to be influential. You also have a greater responsibility, and if you abuse it you can damage your image and your power in the organisation. People gossip about bad chairmen. Everybody finds it frustrating to be at a meeting that is badly chaired. So, if you do chair meetings, make sure that you don't make any of the common mistakes that give a chairman a bad name.

Sort out goals and assumptions

Probably the worst thing you can do when you are in the chair is fail to control the meeting. It is essential for the chair to be clear about the goals of the meeting and to have a plan for achieving them. You need to be quite strong and use group process to control the meeting. First, you need to agree the meeting objectives, and clear up any problems caused by group members having different goals. Discussing goals and assumptions is a good way to start. It focuses minds on the business of the meeting, and saves time later if you sort out mistaken assumptions early on. Even with an explicitly worded agenda people often come to meetings with widely differing assumptions and aims.

Structure the meeting

Once the meeting has agreed where it is going, it is time to plan how to get there. The structure of the meeting will depend on the nature of the decision. You may, for example, be taking a decision on how to develop a new market. A structure for this decision could look like this.

1. Examine all the information that group members have about the new market.
2. Reach agreement on the nature of the new market (eg the socio-economic groups that form the market and where they live and shop).
3. Review what forms of marketing and advertising will best reach this market.

4. Look at the costs of using the most prominent methods of marketing and advertising.

5. Select the most cost-effective method.

6. Develop an implementation plan for tackling the new market. Agree timings, budgets and who is going to do what.

7. Set a date for the next meeting to review progress.

Meetings where there is no plan or structure for decision-making waste time. People chip in with solutions before the problems or background have been analysed. Emotional arguments flare up when decision-making is allowed to be subjective rather than objective. Providing a structure helps everyone to be more disciplined and objective, because it encourages them to base their solutions on a thorough analysis. If people try to jump the gun you can easily remind them that you haven't got to that stage yet. You can delegate to other meeting members some of the meeting tasks like timekeeping, agenda preparation and minute taking. This gives you time to think and contribute. One executive team even has a 'chicken manure' manager whose task it is to point out when they are getting involved in 'minutiae'.

Control by using process

The chair can control the meeting very effectively by using both task and maintenance process. You can, and should, invite people to give information, clarify and summarise. When you spot tensions and difficulties you can use maintenance process to help. Bringing quiet but knowledgeable people into the discussion is particularly useful. To do this you may have politely to ask some of the noisier group members to be quiet for a time. Supporting, encouraging and developing promising ideas will help to create a relaxed and productive atmosphere.

Chairmen who don't use any maintenance process can produce meetings that are very sterile. People don't only bring their brains to meetings, they bring their emotions as well, even though they may try to keep them hidden. An encouraging, supportive chairperson, who keeps good control, optimises ideas, creativity and problem solving.

Avoid adding to the tension and difficulties in the meeting by being negative, indecisive or confused about your own objectives. Negative remarks from the chair are even more powerful than from someone else. If you put people down as chairman, the loss of face can cause them to withdraw for a long time. People respect a good chairman, who states objectives, gathers different views and summarises. The corollary of that is that people won't respect you if you don't do these things.

Don't dominate the meeting

Another common mistake is for the chair to dominate the meeting by talking too much and by being dogmatic about his or her views. The role of the chairman is to use all the ideas and expertise in the room to come to the best decision. If you dominate the meeting, this won't happen. Instead you will get bad decisions and bad feelings. Bad feelings lead to low commitment. You might just find that your decision is not implemented. If you talk for 50 per cent or more of the time then you are dominating the meeting. If you think you have this habit, practise asking questions instead of making statements and ask for views instead of giving your own.

A powerful and secure chairman allows leadership to move around the room. He or she allows meetings to be led, temporarily, by the person who has the greatest stake in, or knowledge about, a particular subject. When this subject is finished with, the chairman reclaims his or her leadership and takes the meeting forward. Insecure chairmen try to prevent this from happening and sometimes leadership struggles occur. This won't do you or the meeting any good. Learn how to view the movement of leadership round the room as a natural occurrence in a well-run meeting, not as a challenge to your power.

Timing

Get the timing right; it's your job if you are in the chair. Good timing shows that you are in control and know what you're doing. Set time scales. If possible, meetings should start at eleven-thirty and only last for an hour. If you are making a decision, don't have too large a meeting. Five or six is the maximum for a good working meeting. Otherwise it will take too long and be less productive. If the meeting is just for exchanging information then you can manage up to twelve people.

Meetings tend to be unproductive after two hours. But make sure when you are planning the agenda that you don't set the meeting a task that is too long to accomplish in the time available. It would be better to plan two separate meetings than to try to make the meeting drag on too long. When people are tired they don't make good decisions.

Make sure the meeting leads to action

Action minutes are a valuable tool for ensuring that decisions get implemented. Against every decision put the name of the person who is going to implement together with the deadline date. Circulate the action minutes after the meeting, and again just before the next meeting. Do everything you can to remind and encourage people to do what they have committed to. You will be exposed as a weak chair if it is discovered at a subsequent meeting that many of the decisions were not implemented.

People need to see action out of a meeting. It reduces your effectiveness if you chair meetings and people don't see action out of them. People will also see you as less than powerful if the meetings you chair do not lead to action.

The theme of this chapter has been to use meetings as a way of increasing your influence and power. Become skilled at using group process because it is an excellent way of increasing your influence by making allies rather than enemies, and creating light rather than heat.

CHAPTER 8

USING POWER TO EMPOWER OTHERS

Managers should make their subordinates more powerful, not less. You can either use your power to empower other people, to enable them to achieve and grow, or you can use your power to disempower, to rob others of power. The latter is the act of the insecure or unskilled manager. Of course, you do need to become powerful to be a successful manager, but it is unwise to try to do this at the expense of other people. Robbing your subordinates of power is not good management. Managers need power to achieve goals and to manage the complicated, contradictory and unwieldy organisation. But this is *not* power in the sense of personal aggrandisement. Subordinates are quick to sense and resent leaders who seek power for personal gain, at others' expense – who are self-important, unapproachable and on the make.

History presents us with examples of ruthless, self-important leaders who have grasped for and won power for themselves, who have terrorised and diminished their subordinates. Some of these people have accomplished great things. Such strategies can be successful, but they are less likely to work in a modern, diffused organisation, with entrenched professionals and a reliance on technical expertise and co-ordination. Your subordinates need to have some power themselves in order to get things done and to achieve results. Empowering others simply means allowing them to use whatever power they have to take action. All too often you see examples of junior staff who are powerless to act or take decisions for themselves. Usually this creates an inefficient and slow-moving department. It's not good for the powerless subordinates, and it's not good for your reputation as a manager. Misusing your power to deny power to others is a short-term strategy only; in the long term it erodes your power base and limits the growth of your own power.

As John Mills says:

My power base comes from my people, it comes from their strengths. My power would soon be undermined if I did not handle my people properly. I prefer to empower people. I like to give them more responsibility because I find that they can take it. If you bring them along with you, and help them to develop as you develop, they will be very loyal to you.

WHY EMPOWER OTHER PEOPLE?

When you enable the people who work for you to become more powerful you build up your own power by:

- making your subordinates loyal to you;
- energising your subordinates;
- increasing their motivation;
- increasing their opportunities for learning;
- increasing performance;
- getting more done, getting better results;
- getting better people to work for you; and
- growing your successor.

When you allow your people to do jobs *their* way, to make their own decisions and learn from their mistakes, you empower them. There is nothing more productive of loyalty, motivation and growth than to know that your manager trusts you to get results your own way. The biggest complaint I hear in organisations I deal with is about managers who can't let go. Managers who play their cards close to their chest, don't trust their subordinates, check on every detail and make all the decisions themselves are very unpopular. They cause resentment by always looking over people's shoulders. They stifle growth and initiative. People can't innovate or think for themselves in such an atmosphere. Therefore, they don't learn and develop. These subordinates have little power. This sort of manager, by being overly concerned with checking and fussing, actually lowers instead of increases performance. Such managers, by stifling initiative and innovation, make it difficult for their departments to respond to change. They therefore damage the long-term future of their departments or companies. High-quality people, wherever they have the choice, will seek to work for managers who give them power, because power is important to their quality of life, as well as to their performance. Thus, managers who allow others to have power end up with the best people.

Most of the managers I interviewed said that using power positively to empower others was a management strategy that produced good results. Tony Hughes says:

> Empowering people will be the key to achieving results in the next decade. We managers have been arrogant in the past in assuming that we know what employees want from work instead of asking them. In studies on the quality of working life the highest values are given to recognition, communication and feedback, *not* pay and conditions as we have seen.

Giving power to your staff not only improves performance, but it speeds up their development. For these reasons, Jerry Stockbridge sees empowerment as a practical approach to management.

> Empowering others is the most essential thing in management. Managers should empower others to achieve results by *their* methods, not the manager's methods. People learn so much if you manage them like this. You let them do the job their way, and let them make mistakes. They will learn from the mistakes and from the successes too.

Roger French also prefers to give other people power and freedom.

> It enables you to get more done. I prefer to play a facilitating role. I organise funding, help my staff to set up the project, create a network and then let them get on with it. Managing in this way also develops people so that you can grow something good in the company. It enables you to get better people. To give power away you've got to be confident and non-vulnerable. You've got to have good relations and trust in your staff.

Tom Nell finds that giving power to other people motivates them.

> I start with the premise that most folk work at 90 per cent of what they can do. If you find a way of switching them on you can help them up to 110 per cent. The hard business reason for giving power to others is the extra 10 or 20 per cent of effort; this is what makes businesses successful, and at the same time people get a kick out of achievement and become successful. It does not always need extra hours. If you do empower people

you'll grow a successor. The absence of a successor is a limit to your progress.

Giving power to your staff also gives you organisational strength. Letting power go downwards generates loyalty from below. For example, when people try to undermine you and take your staff, the loyal ones will warn you of the danger. Insecure managers are afraid to delegate and empower because they fear losing power and status through doing so. Yet, in practice, the opposite happens. Giving power to others creates loyalty and good results, so managers who do this get strengthened, while managers who don't do it lose out.

MANAGEMENT STYLE

Empowerment is a state of mind, and it is also a result of management policies and practices. If the management style in an organisation is about keeping the power at the top, having strict checks and controls, and the assumption that people need close supervision to get results, then you will produce powerless people who don't give everything they've got.

To get motivation managers must give others the power to translate intention into action – and sustain it. People have to feel responsible for their own quality and results. This doesn't mean that managers must *relinquish* power or that subordinates must continuously challenge authority. The 'pull' style of influence is more likely to empower people than the more directive 'push' style. A 'pull' style of influence works by attracting and energising people with an exciting vision of the future. It motivates by identification, rather than through rewards and punishments.

HOW TO EMPOWER PEOPLE

Consensus

One practical way of giving power to your subordinates is to get your team to make decisions through consensus. Keith Manning uses consensus to empower his team.

By going for consensus with my team I get many more ideas than I would working on my own. I get the group to generate ideas, and then modify them and select the best. This works well as long as the discussion is not too emotional and political. When the discussion gets too emotional I have to deal with it by being light and by bringing it back to business goals. I ask people – is your suggestion supportive of what you're trying to achieve?

So Keith empowers his team by helping them to reach consensus. He doesn't dominate the decision-making, neither does he abdicate his leadership. He stays in there and helps with 'group process', which is the way that the group comes to its decisions. When they are having difficulties he uses his skills to put them back on track. When a minority disagree with the decision he ensures that the group as a whole listens to their objections, and either modifies the decisions, or explains why the majority thinks it is for the best.

If you manage the emotional temperature, you get team members to contribute well. You will find that by using this method you get commitment from everyone, even from those who don't agree with the final decision.

Team work

Tom Nell also gives power to his staff by getting them to work in teams to make decisions and solve problems.

I make sure that they know that what they are doing is valued and appreciated, and that they have an influence over things. I encourage them to enjoy their team work and to have some fun, but I also try to let them feel the value of their contribution and sharing in the successes. To motivate them I build a vision of what we're trying to achieve and then manage the team work to make sure it happens. My team buys the vision and ends up working enthusiastically, effectively and at times very long hours, but they enjoy it.

I show an interest in each person on the team, find out about their skills and then demand those skills from them. As a group leader I try to get my team to learn about group process [the way the group works to come to its decisions], and to contribute towards managing the group process. You'll never give power to the group if you just stick to task and technical skills, because it's the process skills that empower. Whitbread have done a lot of empowering by teaching people about group process (on training courses) and letting them share in it. I also insist that the team buys into what we're trying to achieve, and ask them to express any concerns they have at an early stage when there is still a chance to influence the final decision.

Getting people to work in groups is empowering if you manage it so that they feel they will be successful together, and that each one of them has a role to play. Even if some people are not committed to the task, I make sure that they are committed to ensuring that the process is good. I set and share standards, and get them to do work on that together. The standards will be about results, the depth of the work and behaviour. Another way of giving power to your team is allow them to work when you're not there. If you ensure that they are clear about where they are going, you can pull out and let them do it without you. This means I move from being the group's manager to being their consultant, while they manage themselves. Then I am there to support, counsel, get resources and help with my skills if I am asked.

When you do this you are working yourself out of a job, which can be risky in a rapidly changing organisation. However, if you really give power to folk they don't abuse it. The key thing is that your team succeeds and that you're seen to continue to add value to the team. The risk is that they develop so well that they can do without you. But by the time this happens I've had time to think about new opportunities for work so I stay a leap ahead of them and lead them to new levels of success.

Establishing success criteria for the team

There is nothing quite so empowering as success. For your team to be successful they must be clear about what success means. Your team will be working to satisfy the needs and expectations of people outside the team, like customers, users in other departments or senior managers. These people will generate multiple and often conflicting demands on the team, and it is your role as manager to identify the key people involved and to negotiate success criteria with them. You should then let the team know exactly what you have negotiated, so that the team members understand and accept responsibility for achieving a task with clear standards.

Success criteria will consist of the following.

- *Quantitative standards*. These are to do with *the what*. They are objective, measurable standards relating to time, cost, resources and technical criteria.

- *Qualitative standards*. These are to do with *the how*, that is, how the task is going to be carried out. These cover the attitude, skills and behaviour of the team and its members.
- *Targets*. These will be short-term targets about doing new things or achieving new standards.

The Borg Warner case⁷

Here is an example to show how it can work. Self-managing teams, designed to give power to the team members, were set up in the transmission systems division of Borg Warner in South Wales in the 1980s. This is a US-owned international company. The plant in South Wales produces gear boxes, mainly for Saab Motor Company. The company was in trouble at the start of the project and was under threat of closure because of losses. A new managing director took over, who decided, with the aid of external consultants, to bring the company round, by empowering managers and workers to take responsibility for results.

The empowerment project started with management teams, and was cascaded down to the shop floor. The plant was divided into areas. The area supervisor and representatives from each of the nine or ten teams in the area sat on the area board. Each area board, in conjunction with senior management, set targets for each month in production, scrap and quality.

Each team started the month with measures set by the board. The quantitative measures were about the efficiency of labour. The work study department calculated the standard time for each job. The efficiency of labour measured the actual time against the standard time. Other quantitative measures included scrap rates, quality (as measured by the number of warranty claims), operating budgets, absence, lateness and effectiveness. Effectiveness was about making the right component for the right people or departments at the right time.

The qualitative measures were about attitudes which could not be quantified. A climate survey of the workforce was taken every four months, which identified tangible changes in morale. It measured:

- attitude towards the future of the business;
- satisfaction with managers and management style;
- satisfaction with the way production was organised;
- communication.

The short-term targets were those set by each team every month. They would look at the targets set by the area board and decide for themselves in which areas they could do better.

The results obtained by this project over three years were very impressive. There was resistance at first and a long learning curve, yet on every measure there was significant improvement. Operating losses were turned into profits and the plant won a prize from Borg Warner for achieving the greatest reduction in operating costs for the whole company world-wide.

Quantitative results (over three years)
There was a 40 per cent reduction in the cost of production. Quality was increased by 25 per cent. Absence levels fell from 6 per cent to under 1 per cent. Output and yield were up 20 per cent.

Qualitative measures (over three years)
The attitude towards the future of the business went from uncertain to reasonably certain. At the start of the project there had been very low satisfaction with the management, who were seen as corrupt and incompetent people who treated the workers like button pushers. This changed for the better, to a position of trust in management competence. At the start of the project workers thought that managers had lost control. This changed to high and sustained levels of confidence in management. Workers were also more satisfied with the way production was organised. Satisfaction with management communication also improved from 'we are always kept in the dark' to 'communication is consistent and coherent'.

Communicating results
The results identified by these measures need to be communicated to the teams. At Borg Warner the managing director had periodic meetings with the workforce in groups of fifty people. He told them the results and answered their questions. As the company began to do better, this information was very motivating for the workforce, who felt responsible for the improvements.

Partnership

Martin Smith has found that the best way to motivate high-quality staff, and to give them power is through creating a partnership.

What works is creating a partnership environment even at junior levels rather than a boss/subordinate relationship. This creates a positive atmosphere of motivation rather than a negative one. Fear does not work as a motivator. When someone underperforms it is usually because they have negative feelings about themselves. Then you must act as a counsellor. Phoenix is now run on a partnership basis. We pay everyone, including the secretaries, on a performance basis. As a result, they feel part of the whole thing. We have open communications and no secrets. By moving away from continuous short-term evaluation (which doesn't work), to developing a true partnership over the longer term, we have succeeded in building a very valuable business.

Martin found that partnership only works to give power to staff if it is a genuine partnership, and everyone has a stake in the success of the organisation.

At Citibank and Bankers Trust it was very competitive. Top management did say to us – you'll do better if you co-operate and develop a team spirit – but the atmosphere remained competitive. You can create a veneer of partnership in such circumstances, but it can only be skin deep. Your team work and partnerships eventually get challenged, and self-interest comes to the fore again. Then it all breaks up as everyone has to look after themselves and turn to their sponsors for protection.

Ground rules for delegating responsibility

Delegating responsibilities to your subordinates will only work if they are clear about what they are doing, and have guidance from you on the rules and constraints. Delegation without guidelines can lead to confusion or even paralysis. It is very helpful to set ground rules: this will work, this won't, these are the boundaries, here is the goal. Tell your subordinates how you will support them in achieving the goal. If they challenge the goal or suggest a new option, say 'you decide'. You could give advice on whether or not their decision is too risky, but, in the end make it clear that it is *their* decision. At the start of a project agree a number of things with the group:

- exactly what they are doing;
- how you can support their work;
- who and what they need access to and how you can arrange that.

Then you should simply reinforce the work that they do.

The secret of effective and empowering delegation is to be systematic about it. Establish success criteria, targets and deadlines, but also monitor and control while the work is in progress. You may be able to give power to your team by getting *them* to monitor and control, but you must agree clearly with them at the start just how this is going to be done.

Effective control is based on accountability and performance standards, as we saw in the Borg Warner case. The teams knew their standards and were accountable for achieving them, or exceeding them. Quantifiable standards are easier to measure, but don't lose heart if the standards in your work are not quantifiable. If this is so you still need to plan and control performance, so you have to use subjective measurements. When using subjective measures you must first clarify and agree them with your team. Your people will only respond to subjective measurements if they understand and are committed to them.

Choosing the right standard is essential for controlling delegation. What you measure is what you get. You must also ensure that your staff or workers have control over their performance standards. If you use a standard like customer satisfaction for control, and the results are largely determined by whether the transport department delivers on time, you've got a problem. The people in the production department will not feel that they are responsible for achieving performance standards measured in this way.

At the start of delegation you must plan with your team to ensure success and understanding. You must get together to:

- identify results;
- gain commitment to these results;
- anticipate pitfalls;
- identify control standards for performance;
- broadly outline how to approach the job; and
- identify what resources they need.

To prepare for the delegated task you must:

- put the controls into place;
- communicate intended changes;
- allocate resources; and
- schedule activities.

When you have done this planning and preparation you then need only manage by exception. If the controls are agreed and working, the team will be able to see for themselves if they are off target. They only need to report back to you on significant deviations from the plan or anticipated results. Careful preparation empowers, because it gives people the chance to manage themselves, and to be accountable for results without frequent interference from you.

Using delegation in this way to give power to people depends on their maturity and competence to do the work. If they are not up to scratch you will have to coach them in the early days, and help them to anticipate and overcome problems. You should release authority gradually as the person grows in his or her competence and confidence. Too many managers say, 'I can't delegate or release authority because my people just don't want the responsibility.' Of course they don't want the responsibility if they haven't the skill, experience or confidence to tackle the work on their own. Your role as an empowering manager is gradually to help them develop that competence, and to support them through the learning curve.

When you have delegated a task make sure that you evaluate and discuss performance at the end. People need to know if their work was good, and they also need you to help them to learn from their mistakes.

Support

Giving support to people at critical stages in their careers is a very effective way of increasing their power. Rosie Harris feels good about the support she gave to a colleague, thus enabling her to grow in power and status.

> When I set up an internal consultancy within the Prudential I wanted an actuary to work for me. I recruited a woman whom I saw as having potential, but who was unhappy in her present job. She had a first-class honours degree in maths from Oxford, but was doing a job that under-used her skills. I took her on and gave her more and more responsibility and really tested her. She just blossomed.
>
> Later on she came to me and said that she wanted to have a baby, how did I feel about it? I encouraged her and said that we would manage it. When she got pregnant I supported her, as her manager, all the way through it. Now she is on maternity leave. I got a computer terminal put into her home so that she could be more flexible both before and after the arrival of the baby. I telephoned her recently and told her she could be in charge of a department when she returned to work, if she wanted it. She said 'yes' with great enthusiasm.

> My support has done a lot to increase this person's power. In three years she changed from having a position of no authority to running my key department *and* bringing up a baby.

As a result of spotting this woman's potential, supporting her and giving her more power, Rosie has actually increased her own power. She now has a very able, highly motivated and loyal manager working for her, who will strengthen Rosie's power base by producing excellent work. As you empower and develop people, so you enhance your department and your own reputation.

Give people the power to give rewards and incentives

So often we find, lower down in organisations, that staff have to bide strictly by the rules, and have no power to use their judgement or make decisions over 'grey' areas. It is very disempowering to have to refer every complicated decision to your boss, and to have no freedom to use your own judgement or initiative. Having such powerless people working in a service function can be disastrous. Their wooden, churlish unhelpfulness can really reduce customer care.

Tony Hughes, in the restaurant division of Whitbread, has found a way to give increased power to the staff so that service is enhanced.

> In TGI Fridays I made it a golden rule that all waitresses had the power to give three free sweets, and all bartenders could give away four free drinks. This was a way of attracting new people to return to the restaurant.
>
> It has a good effect on the customers, but it has an even *bigger* effect on the staff. It transforms them into hosts and hostesses. It motivates and empowers them. The more you go up the management ladder the more you must give power to the people underneath you. Power energises people. When I give power to people they work with me rather than for me.

DISADVANTAGES OF EMPOWERING OTHERS

However, there are disadvantages in giving power to your subordinates, and you need to be aware of these so that you can plan to overcome them. Keith Manning's point of view is that consensus takes longer and is much harder work.

If I manage an all-day meeting I am drained at the end. The danger, especially if you don't dominate the meeting, is that people may feel for a time that they are not being properly directed. I learnt in the end how to manage these meetings so that this didn't happen.

If you manage by consensus when you have a traditional boss there can be problems. Sometimes, after a day of hard group work I would go with the decision to the boss and he would say 'no'! When I took this negative decision back to the group they got mad because they thought they had wasted their time. In the end, in spite of the disadvantages, we got very good results through our team work.

Keith found that by living with the disadvantages and sticking with his consensus method of making decisions, he got good results, far better than those he would have got, had he not empowered his subordinates to contribute with their skills and knowledge.

Dangers and difficulties in empowering others

When you empower other people you take a risk. Several negative things can happen as a result. You may find that what you are doing is counter to the organisational culture if you work in a very traditional company. Your decision to delegate power may threaten your colleagues and bosses. They may fear that you will lose control. They may also feel challenged by your excellent results and by your success in attracting the best people into your department. If you don't have a strong network and powerful sponsors you could lose out politically to the people you challenge.

Another danger may come from those very staff you have empowered. A manager of an engineering consultancy had this story to tell:

We believed that for the company to grow we needed another level of management under the top directors. We promoted people to this position under us, and gave them a power base. I relinquished some of my power and controls to them. They took this power and within six months I had lost contact with all my clients. These managers took over all client liaison, and built their own power bases with their staff. This left me out in the cold.

Keith Manning also found that involving his staff in decision-making brought him into danger with a traditional boss.

> Even though we exceeded our targets by using the consensus method and empowering everyone to contribute, in the end it cost me my job. I was removed from my job because my boss didn't like my approach. I used to get into trouble with timing because of using the team for consensus decisions. My boss didn't believe in consensus. He felt I wasn't in control of my group.

The excellent performance by Keith's department did not keep him his job. His methods were threatening to his boss, so he lost out for political reasons. However, Keith did not lose out permanently. He still believes in using consensus management to empower his people, in spite of the political difficulties it brought him. Keith thinks that you should stick with what you believe in, and continue to contribute positively. Political environments do change, and now he has been promoted to the management committee. In the end, Keith did not have to sacrifice his beliefs in order to gain that promotion.

The Borg Warner case

Even though giving power to the task groups worked wonders for this organisation, there were many difficulties to overcome. There was a learning curve of about three years, and output had to be sacrificed in the early days while both managers and workers were adjusting to their new powers and responsibilities. The issue was one of trust. The shop floor did not trust senior management initially, and senior managers did not trust each other. For senior managers, the lack of trust took the form of damaging politics, and it took a while for them to build this trust.

The people on the shop floor resisted because they lacked the confidence and competence to take responsibility for managing themselves. Although questionnaires had established that shop-floor workers wanted to make their own decisions, when they were actually given this freedom they backed away from it. At first they had to be managed in a directive way. They were told their targets and also who should do which job in each team. As they became more confident about meeting targets, they began to manage themselves, and make their own decisions about how to tackle jobs, and how to rotate jobs among team members.

There were problems in managing the freedom to make decisions. As the teams became more confident, they wanted to make their own decisions about everything. When their managers had to limit this freedom to a certain extent it caused resentment. Eventually a manual was produced which made it very clear just what the teams could make their own decisions about, and what they could not.

Another early difficulty on the teams was that the workers were unwilling to police each other over effort, lateness or absenteeism. Eventually they began to do this as the connection between their efficiency and company results became clear. Finally, the teams became involved in selecting new members.

The manager who is organising his teams in such a way can come under a lot of pressure. His bosses will be very interested in performance and results in the short term. He will have to do a selling job with senior managers to get them to allow his people to go through a learning curve before the figures start to improve.

BUILD IN SAFEGUARDS

Don't let the dangers and difficulties of empowering people stop you from doing it. The advantages far outweigh the disadvantages. The clever manager does what she thinks is right, and then anticipates danger and builds in safeguards. Your main safeguard will always be to maintain powerful contacts and sponsors who can defend you when you are in trouble or give you other opportunities if you lose your job.

Delegating can take some of your power away. You've got to learn to delegate without abdicating. You've got to keep some decision-making for yourself, and keep controls in place. Ensure that certain decisions cannot be made without your input.

The results you get from increasing the power of your people far outweigh the results gained from close supervision and breathing down their necks. Yet everything that is worth achieving carries a risk. Anticipate the risks and problems if you plan to manage by empowering people, and plan how to deal with them. You may have barriers inside your own head to deal with. It's a popular myth that power is about hogging information and decision-making. It may make you feel power-less and threatened at first when you start to let go. If you want good results do it, but do it properly, with safeguards in place. In the end it will make you, and your people, more powerful.

CHAPTER · 9

DEVELOPING PERSONAL POWER

Assertive behaviour is the key to developing personal power. Aggressive people can be personally powerful too, but this power, being negative, is often counterproductive. Passive people have very little personal power and influence. Even if you are a little cog in a big wheel, you can have personal power. People with personal power are much more likely to be given opportunities to become big cogs, so assertive behaviour helps you to increase your organisational power, as well as your personal power.

The way you deal with people as a manager is crucial to your effectiveness. Managers are always having to cope with problems they have not anticipated. There is no such thing in a management job as doing everything right. Mangers are always vulnerable to internal guilt and external criticism. Other managers can often be highly critical because they may have different values and goals. As a manager you must be satisfied with imperfection and a gradual progress towards goals. If you start the day with a fixed idea of what should happen, feel resentment towards deviations from plans and intolerance towards any failure to achieve plans – this is a path towards ulcers! You may be tempted to lash out against anyone who appears to be blocking your progress.

On the other hand, you may be eager to be accepted by your subordinates and colleagues. But if you let this make you fearful of hostility, and hesitate to confront and correct, you will be ineffective in a world of conflicting goals and interests. Managers cannot expect to be loved. They sometimes need to discipline, refuse requests and place constraints on people.

Somewhere in all of these problems and pressures, you have to find a

138

style of behaviour which enables you to solve problems, stand up for what you think is right, and maintain commitment and co-operation. Developing assertion and personal power will help you to succeed with immediate issues, as well as longer term career goals. This chapter looks at the people skills, in particular the assertion techniques, which you need for a manager's job.

When you are dealing with other people there are four main types of behaviour which you can use.

AGGRESSIVE BEHAVIOUR

Aggressive behaviour involves standing up for yourself at the expense of other people. The aggressive manager does not respect other people, and puts them down or dominates them, without allowing himself to be influenced.

Aggressive behaviour can have short-term advantages

You may, if you are aggressive, get timid or less powerful people to do what you want them to do. Sometimes the shock tactic of suddenly shouting at someone may create movement when hours of gentle persuasion have failed. Aggressive people can also feel powerful, especially when they see their subordinates fearfully scurrying around doing their bidding. However, these advantages rarely last. People will resent you because no one likes to be treated as if their needs don't count. They will be motivated to retaliate, either openly aggressively or indirectly and manipulatively. You are therefore unlikely to get and keep what you want in the long term.

Rosie Faunch tells of her reaction to aggressive behaviour.

I had a colleague who only used to get in touch when something was wrong. He would either phone up and shout at me, or come to see me and behave very aggressively. He would march in, past the secretary, red in the face, demanding to see me and demanding the things that he wanted. I responded to that by trying to delay his requests, even though they were mostly quite reasonable. It was the delivery that I objected to, not what he was actually asking for. I so disliked this treatment that I used the sort of delaying tactics with him that I would castigate in another manager.

Managers are often aggressive when they feel threatened or insecure. However justifiable the causes of aggression, in the end it reduces your ability to influence. Chances are you will begin to feel ashamed of your behaviour. You may even turn these feelings outwards, and blame others and find yourself hating or mistrusting them. The manager who is always surrounded by people whom he or she considers to be untrustworthy fools and incompetents is likely to be an aggressive manager. That manager is lying in the bed he made.

INDIRECTLY AGGRESSIVE BEHAVIOUR

Indirect aggression is when you put the other person down in subtle, underhand ways. It is used by people who respect neither themselves nor other people. They don't feel strong enough to be open about their anger or disapproval, so they show through their tone of voice, expression or actions that they are feeling negative. They may look and speak coldly, bang desk drawers or be sarcastic.

You can manipulate people with indirect aggression

If you are indirectly aggressive, you may be able to get people to do what you want without having to risk refusal by asking them directly. Your manipulative skills can make you feel 'cleverer' than the other person. However, this approach carries serious disadvantages. There is a risk that people will not understand what you want if you don't make it clear. People hate being manipulated. They will probably spot what you are up to and you will lose their co-operation and respect. You are unlikely to get what you want in the long term. Indirect aggression is the behaviour of a person who lacks power and self-respect. Your attempts to manipulate will signal this lack of power and you are therefore likely to reinforce your powerlessness.

PASSIVE BEHAVIOUR

Passive people don't respect themselves. They assume that other people are more important, so they don't stand up for themselves at all. They express their thoughts and feelings in such a self-effacing manner that they invite other people to ignore them.

Passive behaviour may attract you as the safe, low-risk option

If you act unassertively you may feel more comfortable because you are not risking the pain of people confronting or disliking you. You may choose to be passive just for a quiet life. You may feel virtuous because you are being unselfish and self-sacrificing. The price you pay is that you lose your self-respect. Consistent denial of your needs will lead to a growing loss of self-esteem, frustration and internal tensions. People will take advantage of you if you invite them to by being passive. Denying your needs doesn't make them go away and you will experience a build-up of anger, hurt and stress. You certainly won't be admired by everyone for being self-sacrificing. People admire martyrs initially, but end up resenting them and not respecting them.

ASSERTIVE BEHAVIOUR

Assertive people respect both themselves and other people. They stand up for their own rights and needs, but also respect the rights and needs of others. They gain self-respect without diminishing other people.

Assertive behaviour has more advantages than disadvantages

When you are assertive you risk being refused because you say very clearly what you want. Also, when you state your opinion you risk being disagreed with. So assertive people can risk confrontation with other people. These risks are significantly lower if you are skilled in your assertive behaviour, and remember that assertiveness is about respecting the other person as well as yourself. If you do behave assertively your relationships will survive disagreements. No one can manage properly without saying no, causing disappointment and confrontations. However, if you handle these situations in a way that shows you respect the right of the other person, you reduce the risk and pain.

Assertion is certainly the most influential and satisfying way to behave. People understand clearly what you want and what you stand for. Good leaders make their position clear, and are trusted and followed because they are consistent. Because you respect their needs, your subordinates will not feel browbeaten or manipulated. You will increase your self-respect and win respect from others. You are more likely to get what you want, both in the short term and in the long term. Assertive people are rewarding, approachable, high-energy people. People know where they stand if you say what you want, or what your concerns are, without sarcasm, manipulation or hostility.

Rosie Faunch gives us another example, this time of an assertive colleague.

> One of my managers wrote to me a very helpful and convincing letter explaining how he would like to expand one aspect of his service. He showed that he understood my pressures and was full of empathy. He made it clear that he understood that the cost of his proposal might be a problem and even suggested a source of funding. I phoned back and we sorted it out in ten minutes and he was able to go ahead.

Assertion enhances your management skills

Assertive behaviour in a manager enhances his or her managerial effectiveness. If you look at the personal attributes that makes a manager influential and effective you will see how assertion can give you the skill and courage to be like this. As a manager you need the following.

- The ability to get co-operation, make contacts and work with them to solve problems.
- Perseverance – the ability to keep going back to the same people and raise the same issues, when those issues remain unresolved. You also need to maintain the enthusiasm to persuade, negotiate and propose new possibilities.
- The ability to keep talking in order to present ideas when others want to interrupt and take over.
- Flexibility – the ability to adjust your approach to fit in with other people's ideas or constraints.
- The ability to listen, particularly when a highly emotional or controversial view is being put.
- Equanimity – the ability to stay calm and keep trying when others are unresponsive or aggressive.

If you go through your days fearful of saying 'no', fearful of asking for what you want, or dealing with problem people with a battering ram, you won't be able to develop the personal attributes you need. Assertive managers who develop skills in dealing with others get action and influence. The next section shows how to deal assertively with people, and thus enhance your personal power.

GUIDELINES FOR ASSERTION

Understanding that assertive behaviour is influential and powerful is a start. Here are some guidelines for developing a more assertive leadership style which will help you to deal with people more effectively.[6]

The next time you want to ask for something, try following this sequence:

- give information;
- say what you want;
- point out the benefits; and
- also point out the negative consequences.

When you are doing this, be expressive, let the other person know how you feel and where you stand. Make sure you are clear before you start about what you want and work towards achieving that goal in your discussions. Be as clear as you can, avoid vagueness and inaccuracies. It is possible to inadvertently sound aggressive if you say what you want first, and only give the information and background second, or not at all. See what you think of this example: '*I want you to complete this drawing right away. The client is coming for a meeting in four hours time, and I will need it for our discussions.*

If instead, you gave the relevant information first, *then* said what you wanted, the message would be less demanding and pressurising: '*Our client is coming for a meeting at four o'clock, and we will need to discuss that drawing. I would like you to complete it now so that it can be ready in time.*'

When you have made your request clearly, you may find that the other person raises objections. Avoid putting them down if you have a disagreement. Use 'I' statements like 'I feel' or 'I think'. These work much better than 'you' statements, which sound accusatory and aggressive. Here is another example: '*I find it hard to motivate the rest of the team to start on time when you arrive late.*'

Compare this to a more accusatory 'you' statement: '*You make it hard for me to motivate the others to start on time when you arrive late.*'

The first statement is a more objective statement of the problem, and gives information without putting the other person down.

Assertive managers are brief and to the point. Don't spend too much time giving innumerable reasons and excuses. Just say what you want and think in an honest and open fashion, using a pleasant but firm tone of voice. Then, even when you have something negative to say, people will find it more acceptable. And most of all, be persistent. To show persistence, give your instructions or requests in a tone of voice that shows that you expect attention to be paid to you. Avoid scolding, whining, apologising or rationalising. Behaviour like this shows that you are not sure if you are going to be obeyed, and so invites people to try to ignore you.

Assertive managers have the following key people skills.

- They can accept people as they are, not as they would like them to be. Everyone has strengths and weaknesses and deserves to be respected. The assertive manager is able to remember and respect people's strengths, even when he has to talk to them about their weaknesses.
- Assertive managers treat people close to them with the same courteous attention that they extend to strangers and casual acquaintances.
- Assertive managers trust other people, even if it sometimes feels risky to do so. Although it would be naïve to trust everyone all of the time, it is very bad if you trust no one. People do respond to your trust and confidence in them. The assertive manager is willing to live with the risk of being let down some of the time, because he benefits from being able to trust and respect people.

YOUR ASSERTIVE RIGHTS

Self-respect is fundamental to assertive behaviour. To help you to build your self-respect, try reminding yourself that you have rights as a human being, regardless of who or what you are. Being clear about your rights makes it easier to decide whether you need to stand up for them.

Here is a list of the general rights which everyone has. You have the right to:

- be treated with respect as an intelligent, capable and equal human being;
- have and express opinions, views and ideas which may or may not be different from other people's;
- have these opinions, views and ideas listened to and respected;

- have needs and wants and ask that others respond to them;
- say yes to or refuse a request without feeling guilty or selfish;
- make mistakes;
- change your mind;
- ask for more information;
- decline responsibility for others' problems; and
- decide not to assert yourself (eg choose not to raise a particular issue).

Recognising that you have these rights can be a big help in developing the confidence to stand up for yourself when people are being aggressive towards you. But remember that other people have these rights too and in order to be assertive you must recognise *their* rights.

THE INNER VOICE – THE POWER OF BELIEFS AND FEELINGS

Feelings and emotions often interfere with our ability to act assertively. We all hold internal dialogues inside our heads, and these inner voices influence how we feel and behave. They can play havoc with our effectiveness. Many people are unaware of just how much time they spend in their heads, or of the negative and counterproductive thoughts they entertain. Here are some common effects of these negative thoughts.[8]

- Drawing conclusions on the basis of minimal evidence (eg people will find me a terrible nuisance if I ask a favour).
- Seeing things in black and white, rather than recognising options and shades of grey.
- Exaggeration of problems (eg this problem is so vast and all-encompassing I shall never overcome it).
- Catastrophising (eg if I don't get this promotion it will mean the end of my career).
- Setting rigid limits (eg I must work twelve hours a day or I have to get this 100 per cent right).
- Self-punishment (you idiot – how could you have made such a silly mistake, it was unprofessional of you).
- Labelling yourself negatively (I'm boring, inconsequent, inarticulate, slow).

The best way to deal with this counterproductive inner dialogue is to tune into it and listen to what you are saying to yourself. You need to recognise these voices for what they are: inappropriate, irrational and unreasonable relics from the past. Becoming aware of these inner voices gives you clues as to how you block your own assertion and is the first step in changing. Be prepared to pause and challenge the inner voice – is it really saying something valid and reasonable? Chances are you will see that it is not. Try instead to substitute positive, supportive messages like the following.

- If I don't get this promotion it will be disappointing, but I can learn from the failure if there is one, and plan how to re-route my career path.
- If I ask a favour, chances are people will help if they can, and if they say 'no' it's no big deal, I'll just ask someone else.
- I don't need to get everything 100 per cent right. I know I have the skills to get this nearly right, and if it isn't perfect at least I can learn from any mistakes. It isn't awful to make a mistake.
- It's natural and OK to feel nervous.
- Not everyone has to like or agree with me, but I like and respect myself.

If a conversation with someone goes wrong and you were unable to deal with it assertively, review what the inner voice was saying to you. Don't keep replaying the situation in your head, feeling worse each time. It won't be productive. Just see what you can learn from the failure to be assertive, then put it away and build in positive 'I can' messages for the future.

SOFTENING YOUR STYLE

Assertion has been popular and fashionable since the late 1970s. Many of us have learnt (even if we didn't know before) how to stand up for ourselves and to take care of ourselves. In the rush to make sure that we demand our rights, some of us have lost touch with the fact that assertion is not just about ourselves, it is about the other person too. This is why it is such a useful technique for managers. Any manager, in order to get things done, must tap into the energy, commitment and knowledge of others. If you focus only on your own achievements, your own rights and needs, the chances are that you will end up being *aggressive* when you think you are learning how to be *assertive*.

A good way of avoiding this mistake is to learn how to be responsively assertive. I will contrast responsive assertion with basic assertion. Basic assertion is when you state your needs and opinions in a direct, down-to-earth way, without any frills: 'We have a tight deadline on this report, I would like you to work overtime tonight.'

If your tone of voice is right you are not necessarily violating the rights of the other person. If you are not aggressive or pressurising in your tone there is no reason why your subordinate cannot say: 'I'm sorry to let you down, but I'm going to a concert tonight, so I can't stay beyond 7 pm.'

However, you are his manager, and this does put you in a position of having some power over him. Your subordinate could interpret your statement as an order or a threat whether you meant it that way or not. The problem with basic assertion is that it is open to misinterpretation. If your tone of voice is slightly insistent, or if you are seen as a slightly awesome figure, then the other person may feel as if they are being given no room to manoeuvre. They could feel that they have no rights.

Responsive assertion

This is a way of overcoming the problem of misinterpretation. With this form of assertion you state your needs and check with the other person that you aren't violating theirs. So you would say something like this: 'We have a tight deadline on this report. I would like you to work overtime tonight. How does that fit in with your plans?'

This statement makes it clear that you are inviting the other person to say what they want or if they have a problem. When they tell you their problem you will have to negotiate a compromise. But you have shown clearly that you respect both your needs and theirs, so it is less likely you will be misconstrued as aggressive.

Below is a questionnaire which will help you to decide just how responsive you are in your communication.[9]

Instructions

Below you will find a series of paired statements, an 'A' statement and an 'R' statement. You are asked to distribute ten points between the two statements. You might give all ten points to the A statement and no points to the R statement. This would indicate that the A statement comes closest to describing your behaviour or feelings and the R statement is not at all descriptive. You might give equal points (5 points to A, five points to R) if both statements fit your behaviour about equally. (Or, you might give eight to A and two to R, or four to A and six to R, and so on.) For each question, the number of points for A plus R should equal ten.

PAIRED STATEMENTS

A STATEMENTS	R STATEMENTS
1. I spend more time talking than listening Points _____	I spent more time listening than talking. Points _____
2. When I am under pressure I am usually energised and I inspire other people to act. Points _____	When I am under pressure I am good at paying attention to the feelings of others. Points _____
3. I get results through my energy and strength of personality. Points _____	I get results by stimulating and encouraging other people to put their energies into the task. Points _____
4. I try very hard to ensure that people understand my point of view. Points _____	I try very hard to ensure that I understand other people's views. Points _____
5. I deal with objections and disagreements by trying harder to sell and persuade. Points _____	I deal with disagreements by considering the points made, and answering them or changing my proposal if appropriate. Points _____
6. I am usually the one who initiates ideas in meetings. Points _____	In meetings I tend to be responsive to other people, and build on their ideas. Points _____
7. When I am attacked I stand up for myself and fight back in a straightforward way. Points _____	When I am attacked I try to diffuse the situation by distracting or appeasing the other person. I let them run out of steam. Points _____

8. Sometimes people find me a bit too tough.

Points _____

Sometimes people find me too tolerant and easy-going.

Points _____

9. I am a strong competitor.

Points _____

I am good at co-operation and collaboration.

Points _____

10. I prefer to take the initiative in directing and shaping events. I usually take charge of situations and make suggestions.

Points _____

I prefer to get things done by finding out what other people want and responding to that.

Points _____

11. When I am unhappy with a person's performance I demand that they set goals for improvement, and may even suggest what those goals should be.

Points _____

When I am unhappy with a person's performance I try to understand why they are under-performing and involve that person in setting goals for improvement.

Points _____

12. If I deal badly with poor performance it is usually because I am too abrupt or even hostile.

Points _____

If I deal badly with poor performance it is usually because I give in too easily or am patronising.

Points _____

Total A points _____

Total R points _____

Have a look at your score. If your A score is very high, then you could probably make your communication style more effective by learning how to be more responsive.

Guidelines for responsiveness

Being responsive is really about being explicit about your concern for the other person's needs as well as your own. Invite them to say what they think or want by asking questions or being supportive. Don't just leave it to them to guess by your tone of voice that you wouldn't mind if they say what they think. Show that you are trying to tune into their feelings, their problems or their goals. Try to show empathy and understanding. This is particularly important for managers with a lot of power, either personal or organisational. You do have to put yourself out to show timid or junior people that you are approachable and human. They won't be able to work it out for themselves if they are slightly in awe of you.

A responsive communication style will help you to avoid many of the barriers to downward communication. These are the main barriers:

- selective or inattentive listening;
- selective filtering of information based on the manager's perception of what employees *ought* to be told and *ought not* to be told;
- distorting information through personal values and bias;
- selective filtering of information from above because of expectations that the subordinate will overreact;
- distorting information through colouring it with personal feelings of the moment.

The benefits to you as a manager from becoming responsive and open in your communications are many:

- People will tell you what you need to know to plan ahead and to avert disasters. This will be a real advantage to a manager who normally spends his life responding to crises.
- The free flow of information will give you greater freedom and accuracy in making decisions and greater opportunities for creativity.
- You will have more options in responding to problems. If you invite people to tell you about their problems and actually listen to them, they in turn will be inclined to put themselves out to help you to solve yours.
- You won't avoid problems, but you will have more information about those that do arise.

So by increasing your responsiveness, you increase your effectiveness and information power.

BODY LANGUAGE

Body language is about:

- eye contact;
- facial expressions;
- posture;

- gestures and mannerisms; and
- tone of voice.

This is a very important aspect of assertion, because it signals how you are feeling about yourself and other people. If you say one thing and your body language says another, then it's the message given by your body language that people respond to. They don't believe your words. If, for example, you say: 'My door is always open, I want you to come in whenever you need to talk to me', but every time a subordinate walks in you keep on writing for thirty seconds before looking up, and then look forbidding and unsmiling, you will soon find that your invitation is not taken seriously.

To be assertive you need to manage your body language to ensure that it reinforces rather than contradicts your spoken words.

Posture and distance

Do you stand or sit upright or slouched? A straight back indicates self-respect. Are you too near or too far from the other person? Getting too close can be read as dominating and disrespectful. Are you rigid, or relaxed and alert? The latter posture gives the message that you are in control and feeling open, unthreatened and unthreatening.

Eyes

Is your gaze relaxed and friendly? Do you look people in the eye? An averted gaze signals anything but assertion.

Mouth

Do you hold your jaw tightly? Is your smile appropriate or is it a warning that an attack is on the way? An assertive manager has a relaxed but expressive face which doesn't over-dramatise emotions, neither does it hide them to the extent that his or her face tightens up over the years.

Voice

Watch the tone, inflection and volume. Assertive people neither shout nor speak too quietly. Quiet voices signal unassertiveness, even if the rest of your body language is confident. Try to avoid whining, bellowing, or sarcastic tones. Perhaps you need to work on not being too quietly spoken. Try to project your voice powerfully, perhaps even raising it deliberately sometimes, so that you don't seem too quiet for the situation.

Gestures

We often signal nervousness with our hands and feet. Hands which rub your nose, stroke your hair or jangle keys in pockets show that you are ill at ease. So do shuffling feet. Folded arms can make you look defensive. On the other hand, you don't need to avoid gestures completely. Strong, firm gestures used occasionally denote assertion and power.

Speaking

Do you mumble, hesitate, repeat yourself or swallow your words and leave sentences unfinished? All of these signal unassertiveness. Try to speak clearly and fluently.

Appearance

What impression do you wish to convey to other people? Are you dressed and groomed in a way that signals your influence and assertion? More detail is given in Chapter 11 on managing your image.

Breathing

Deepen your breathing and calm yourself before an assertive confrontation. Noticing your breathing and learning how to relax your body reduces your anxiety and helps you to feel poised and centred, even in a difficult situation. If you would like to make a deeper study of body language, try Michael Argyle's book, *Bodily Communication* (Methuen 1988).

ASSERTIVENESS TECHNIQUES

It is not enough just to say that you should try to be assertive all of the time. Most of us realise that assertive people are more effective and powerful anyway. The problem is how to be assertive in those tricky situations that you don't know how to handle. There are many instances in your life as a manger when you will find yourself acting aggressively or unassertively even though your initial intention was to be assertive. There are assertiveness techniques for handling a lot of these situations. You will find some of these useful.

Making requests

We often hesitate to make requests or ask favours, either because we don't want to impose, or because we fear rejection. Remind yourself that you have a right to ask for what you want or ask for information. It's probably only your inner voice stopping you from doing it. It may also help you to remember that people have the right to refuse a request. If you ask assertively, then you don't interfere with their right to refuse and don't embarrass them or yourself.

Here are some tips:

- don't apologise;
- be direct and brief;
- give a reason if it helps;
- don't oversell; and
- don't hint or ask indirectly.

Saying 'no' without feeling guilty

Managers who cannot say 'no' become overloaded and ineffective. If you say 'no' assertively, there is no reason why you should cause offence. The other person will be disappointed, but if you handle it assertively they won't feel bad about it.

Here are some guidelines for saying no.

- Ask for clarification.
- Make sure you want to say 'no'. If you're not sure, ask for time to think about it.
- Say 'no' clearly and directly. Use the word 'no' in your answer.
- Use empathy because this makes your refusal more acceptable.
- Don't make excuses, but give a brief (genuine) reason.
- Don't apologise profusely. 'I'm sorry' said once will do.
- Offer a compromise if you can think of one, but don't try to take over ownership of the problem.

For example, Bill is asking his manager, Louise, if he can have the day off tomorrow.

'Louise, can I have Friday off please? We are going to France and I would like to make a long weekend of it.'

'I'm sorry Bill, I'll have to say no because two other counter staff are away and we can't do without you.'

'Hey, come on Louise, I'm sure you'll find a way to cope, what's a few more people in the queue anyway? It would really help me out.'

'I realise it would make your travelling much easier, and I regret not being able to help. But I have strict instructions to man four out of the five counter positions and I can't do that tomorrow if you're not here.'

'What a pain!'

'Look, there's no way I can lose you on Friday, but maybe we can think of another way of solving the problem.'

'Great! Have you any ideas?'

'Why not take Monday off instead?'

'That's a thought! Or maybe I could leave at three on Friday when the counters close, and return by eleven on Monday.'

'Whichever suits you best.'

'Thanks Louise, I'll come back in an hour and let you know which one I'll go for.'

Louise made it clear that she was saying no, but kept communication open by using empathy. Had she been aggressive or curt in her refusal she might have had an unpleasant row, and a demotivated employee on Friday. Had she given in and said 'yes' to avoid a row, she would have been in trouble with *her* boss. So saying 'no' assertively was her best option.

Dealing with manipulation

If the other person becomes manipulative when you say 'no', try the *broken record* technique. This technique is marvellously effective in dealing with people who use emotional blackmail, behave deviously and try to hook you with unjustified criticisms, irrelevances or threats. Choose a suitable phrase starting with 'I', and without raising your voice or getting steamed up, repeat this assertive statement every time the person tries to persuade you to change your mind.

If you keep repeating this original statement and resist the temptation to respond to insults, threats and manipulation, you will soon convince the other person that you mean what you say. Broken records do get paid attention to – because it's uncomfortable to listen to them for too long! It's a technique which helps you to stay in control of both the conversation and your emotions. It gives you power in a situation which could otherwise have turned sour, with you losing your temper and getting involved in undignified arguments.

Here is an example of a broken record being played.

'Jim, I just realised that I need those figures by tomorrow.'

'I'm sorry Pat, we have been working towards the original deadline of the end of this week. I can probably let you have them a day early, but even if we all work overtime there is no way we can finish them by tomorrow.'

'Listen, my reputation is at stake here, and so is yours. I can't believe you can't speed things up a bit, you've often done so before.'

'I appreciate that it's a problem. I will get everyone to work overtime and we will finish them a day early, but I can't let you have them tomorrow.'

'Hey, what sort of friend are you anyway? Don't you remember how I helped you out last month? Don't ask me for any help again!'

'Pat, I'm really sorry I can't do more. I'll let you have the figures by Thursday, but tomorrow is too soon.'

'You are a hard man. Can't you see I've got a problem here? I suppose you think it's a self-inflicted wound and that I should live with the consequences.'

'I will do everything I can to speed things up. But I know that tomorrow is impossible. I'm always ready to do anything within reason to help you.'

'Oh well, I guess I'll just have to make do with that. Thanks.'

Another form of manipulation is the person who sheds tears as a way of making you feel guilty and stopping you in your tracks. Rosie Faunch has a way of dealing with manipulative staff which has never let her down.

I let them cry, offer a tissue, say nothing, then when they are finished, get right back to the point and start the discussion again. This is much better than reacting, which would mean that you are letting them draw you into their game. It is, of course, important to distinguish this type of staff from one who is genuinely distressed and needs tender loving care!

Receiving criticism

All managers will get criticised from time to time, you can't avoid it. You can, however, increase your personal power by handling it well. Avoid becoming defensive or engaging in unconstructive arguments:

- listen carefully;
- don't be defensive; and
- distinguish between fair and unfair criticism.

Unfair criticism

If the criticism doesn't matter then don't waste time and energy on dealing with it. Don't bother to deny it, but don't accept it either. Just say things like: 'you may be right' or 'that's a point to consider'.

If the criticism *does* matter then don't wear any caps that don't fit you:

- reply assertively that you do not agree;
- keep calm and neutral, but firm;
- say why you don't agree with it.

Receiving fair criticism

If the criticism is valid, try to remember that you have the right to make a mistake, but that the other person also has a right to complain. Don't be manipulated through guilt or anxiety into either endlessly trying to explain, or seek forgiveness or being defensive. If you do this you will impress no one and feel worse. Just take it in your stride:

- listen carefully to the criticism;
- ask for details;
- apologise and say what you're going to do to put it right.

If you've made a boo-boo, come clean. If possible make a joke of it.

Giving criticism

Managers often dislike criticising, but your subordinates need to know when they are going wrong. You can criticise assertively, in a way that is helpful to the receiver:

- give it soon after the event, but preferably not in public;
- give it in a supportive atmosphere;

- concentrate on things that can be changed;
- describe rather than evaluate;
- use 'I' statements (not 'you' statements);
- look them in the eye; and
- don't whine or shout.

Here is an example of an assertive criticism: 'Peter, I've noticed over the last few weeks that your manner with me has been blunt, and sometimes curt. I know that you have been under a lot of pressure, and that the last thing you may want to think about is human relations! But I do feel put down quite frequently by your behaviour and would prefer a friendlier tone.'

If you give your criticism assertively, you reduce the risk of a defensive or aggressive response, but you don't eliminate that risk. You may still find your criticism challenged as unfair or inaccurate. When this happens give concrete and recent examples to illustrate the point you are making. Three examples is a good, convincing number. Less than three may lead to a 'special circumstance' argument and more than three will be too discouraging.

Discourage and confront passive behaviour

Passive behaviour is a form of withholding. People can use it as a strategy for getting what they want, like help, sympathy and less work. It manipulates us into feeling either guilty or sorry for such people. Remember that even quiet people are never as vulnerable as they appear:

- ask them to tell you what they want;
- explain that it is difficult for you to guess what they want if they don't tell you; and
- be supportive, but make it clear that you don't feel guilty.

Dealing with anger

The most useful strategy for dealing with anger is to distance yourself psychologically and avoid engaging in a row. When there is hostility and anger around it is the person who stays calm and in control who has the power, however abusive the other person is being. Try to understand the problem instead of becoming emotionally involved.

- Listen. Let the angry person get it off their chest. Interruptions or pleas to calm down will just make them angrier.
- Try, by asking questions, to find out why they are angry.
- Don't argue back or appease at this stage, just recognise that they are angry.
- When they have had a chance to express their feelings and cool down, then (and only then) do what you can to deal with the problem. Apologise, explain or discuss solutions.

Remember, you always have the right to walk away if someone is being totally unreasonable.

TAKE YOUR PEOPLE SKILLS SERIOUSLY

The barriers, inconsistencies and frustrations which are part of organisational life can easily lead managers to impatience, anger and resentment. Such emotional reactions, even though understandable, will injure your performance. The people you deal with sense your pent-up or openly expressed hostility, and in turn become less responsive and helpful. They do this either because they resent your emotional display or because they cannot control their own inner stress.

Michael Lainas warns us of the need to manage our emotions.

You have a responsibility as a manager to be positive. Make sure that you manage your emotions so that you are seen as a generator rather than a drain – even when you are down. It is vital in a senior job to be seen as a generator of ideas and relationships. It is not about popularity, but it's about having a powerful personality. You can even be critical in a positive way.

Managers who are frequently depressed and who complain a lot will find that people are not so keen to work for them. It's a real killer to have to spend a lot of time with a negative person.

This chapter has been about developing a powerful personality and positiveness through assertion. Let self-respect and respect for other people be the basis of your management style. It is a way of increasing your power and influence.

CHAPTER 10

HOW TO LOSE GRACEFULLY

Being influential is not just about winning, it's also about handling your failures in a way that maintains your influence. It is dangerous even to *think* that you're going to win all the time. It's good to be positive, optimistic and strategic, but if you don't plan how to deal with failure you may handle it badly, and lose some of your influence and power. This chapter may sound as if it's going to be pessimistic, but it's not. It is about being realistic and about having a positive approach to defeat, accepting that this is an inevitable part of a manager's life.

Certainly, if you acquire sponsors, develop your power base and learn people skills you will be successful more often than not. But you can't win all of the time, even if you are very influential. Even the most energetic, strategic and enthusiastic of the managers I interviewed accepted that you should not expect that things will always go the way you want them to. Yet they were all philosophical about not winning because they saw failure as an inevitable part of becoming more powerful and effective. They accept it, contingency plan for it, learn from it, then go on to success.

You will not be successful if you don't ever expect to fail. You will reduce your failure rate if you look for ways to avoid confrontation. Look for a way around a problem instead of taking it head on. But you must accept that some things won't happen. You're bound to be unsuccessful some of the time. If you don't accept that you will have a percentage of failure, you will have fewer successes and may achieve less.

People who cannot contemplate or cope with failure tend to play it safe and avoid taking risks. In most jobs this approach will lower your achievement and probably frustrate your subordinates. Risk-takers make achievements, but they also have some failures. You should never take a risk you can't afford to lose, but you should also not let fear of failure hold you back from achieving.

Try to avoid seeing things as winning or losing. You should see occasional failures as part of your strategy for success and learn from the failures. There is a lot of learning to be had from losing. Focus your energy into analysing the loss for the next time.

HANDLING DEFEAT

It will help you to cope with defeat if you have a positive approach towards dealing with it. You should make contingency plans for dealing with failure right from the start. While you're fighting the battle, give some thought to the question – what if I don't win?

Jerry Stockbridge has a very good approach towards failing.

> It doesn't work to crow about success. By the same token, if you fail, have a runners up party! But don't take coming second all of the time. It is important to understand *why* a thing succeeded, and also *why* it failed. Ultimate failure is failure to learn.

Having a runners up party may not work in all organisations, but the philosophy behind it is don't get bogged down in defeat. Don't be sour-faced and ungracious about it.

Losing a battle may only be a temporary setback in winning a war, but losing noisily and with bad grace may cause you to lose the war as well. You won't be seen as powerful and as having potential for senior jobs if you can't handle your emotions in defeat. An emotional oversell can make you fail at a meeting, because you will be seen as lacking perspective. In just the same way, managers who are angry and ungracious in defeat are seen as lacking the necessary balance, perspective and maturity. Don't burn any bridges behind you. Remember, an influential manager's life is a constant effort to build contacts, so don't destroy your previous good work through the way you handle a failure.

It helps if you put yourself into the shoes of the decision-maker and try to work out why they had to say no. This will give you the balance and perspective you need to cope with your disappointment. For example, when a company is under severe commercial pressure management tasks become short term. If you try to win an argument about doing something strategic and long term you won't succeed. The debate about strategy becomes an irritant when the company needs to be focused on this month's cash flow. There won't be a long term if you don't pay attention to the short term.

Even if you've been unfairly treated, and it is obvious to everyone that this is so, you've still got to handle the defeat with dignity, or else you will start losing sympathy. Keith Manning had to deal with a big defeat when he lost his job as sales director because his boss didn't like his consensus approach.

> You've got to feel laid-back about what happened to you personally. When I lost my job as sales director of the Metropolitan region I protested too much *emotionally* to the chief executive. I think he saw me as overemotional. However, I didn't burn any bridges with the boss who had sacked me. When I was transferred I went to see my old boss and said – How can I help you in my new job?

While there is still a chance that you can turn things back in your favour, then you must keep fighting. However, once it is clear that you have lost, then even though you may want to make your disappointment clear, do so briefly and then accept your defeat. You can't expect to win all the time. Once you've lost, stop arguing. When the organisation has made a decision, they don't want people chipping away at the sidelines saying, 'That was wrong.' See it as a battle lost, and think about how to win the war.

Rosie Harris was coping with a difficult defeat when I interviewed her.

> I was given the job of financial controller with a promise of promotion to assistant general manager level. I've recently been told that I am not going to be promoted to this job as assistant general manager. They are going to put someone in over me instead of promoting me to do the job. This leaves me with the responsibility but not the status. I can't stop it happening, it's been decided already. I was told the reason was that I was too young.
>
> I was devastated when I heard the news. My unhappiness showed. Every board member noticed and came to see me to cheer me up and encourage me to stay. I didn't get overemotional about it. I just made it clear that I was disappointed. It was tough to cope with because everyone had expected me to be promoted, and suddenly I wasn't going to be anymore.

Rosie then settled down to review the situation and decide what to do.

> One senior person talked to me about it and said that it wasn't because I was female. I reflected on it and decided that they couldn't cope with me being young *and* female.

Rosie obviously wondered whether the decision had been made because she wasn't doing her job well enough. She used her large network to establish that she was seen as doing a good job, so she took heart from that. She used her network to talk things over and to help her to decide the way forward. Senior contacts have told her that there are a number of rewarding senior jobs that she could do in the Prudential. So by handling the problem with dignity, she has kept her allies, been able to make her disappointment clear, and receive support and encouragement. If Rosie stays with the company, people won't forget how she handled this setback. She will go on to win the war. Indeed, soon after Rosie was offered a new job as business operations manager, reporting to the sales director. She was pleased to accept because this is a broader based operational role and an even higher profile job than the previous one.

Don't let your gracious handling of defeat stop you from making your disapproval or disappointment clear. You want the decision-makers to register your point of view, even if they are not going to bide by it this time. If it turns out that the decision was wrong, then it helps your image if you made it clear originally that it wasn't what you would have chosen.

For example, one way of losing, of course, is to be excluded. Perhaps then you could go to the decision-makers and say, 'You should have included us, you'll have to go back to Stage One and bring us in.' You have to make a stand sometimes, but only if you can add practical value. It's worth making a stand to ensure that they're not tempted to do it to you again.

Judging when the decision is final

If it is a good strategy to fight, while there is still a chance, and then accept defeat when the decision is final, then you must learn to judge *when* that decision is final. At meetings with majority votes it is usually quite clear, but at meetings where consensus decisions are made it is not so easy to tell. But when the chairman announces the decision, minutes it and moves on to the next item of the agenda, then you can assume that it is all over. If the decision is taken by an individual, or by a meeting that you haven't attended, then you can assume finality when the decision is made public. If the decision is a result of a discussion between you and your boss, then you can usually tell by the finality of his tone of voice that the time for argument is over. Learn to judge, because mistakes will cost you.

Occasionally it pays to make a fuss

You can use anger to good effect when facing the danger of possible defeat. There are people who hate rows and scenes, and they may give in simply because they haven't the stomach for your anger. Some leaders use anger and argument deliberately. It is usually not effective when you *know* you've lost, unless you want to make it clear what you've lost and what compensation you need in terms of future favours. There is a danger in giving in too easily because people may not realise that it has hurt you. It can be poor advice to tell people to dampen their emotions. It's better to channel them and make them work for you. Anger can make people want to appease you.

Although strong emotions can be made to work for you in some situations, it is usually preferable to express your anger and disappointment assertively. Aggression has short-term effects sometimes, but is usually counterproductive in the end. If you are too frequently enraged by your failures you could risk being written off as bad tempered and immature.

TURNING DEFEAT INTO VICTORY

If you see that things aren't going your way, sometimes a strategic rethink or withdrawal can preserve your chances of victory in the future.

Rosie Harris managed to turn a spectacular failure into just as big a success.

When I was an auditor at Deloittes, one of my clients was a health authority. I had to do a job that I wasn't qualified to do, but I didn't have any choice so I attempted it. It was an uphill struggle because not only was I unqualified, but the doctors did not think that auditors should be involved in the project. When I presented my work it was ripped apart by the treasurer of the health authority. I was faced with having to redo the work.

Rosie could have been paralysed by such a public failure, or she could have decided to look for an escape route and blame Deloittes for throwing her to the lions in such a way. But she didn't take that point of view.

I decided to approach it as a personal challenge. I wanted to mend my reputation by turning a failure into a success. So I had to rethink my work and make sure that it was acceptable when I presented it the second time. It was very hard to do, but I managed it. The second instalment was a great success.

Mike Dearden found that strategic and timely withdrawal brought success for his project.

I don't force issues that I am in danger of losing. Once I took a proposal to my boss and got a 'no', but not a clear 'no'. When I saw in my meeting that I wasn't going to win, I asked him to let me withdraw and rethink my presentation. He agreed.

After the meeting I probed informally in the network to discover why he had resisted my proposal. I learned that a reorganisation was in the wings that I had not known about. This affected my case so I held fire for a while. Four months later I got information from the field which indicated that a problem existed out there that my proposal would have solved. I went back to my boss in private, put the new evidence and argued my case again. This time I got 70 per cent of what I wanted. If I had pushed at the first meeting I would have got a firm 'no' and I would not have been able to go back and reopen the case.

You often get another chance

Even if you lose your case today, don't feel that you have lost forever. Just bide your time and keep your proposal on ice. The likelihood is that you will get another opportunity, as long as your proposal is sound.

John Mills has this to say:

When I lose, my public stance is to say – it's not my advice, but I will try my best to get it to work. Internally, I just bide my time and know that we will have this argument again in eighteen months. You have got to console yourself with the fact that you are right and that sooner or later it'll come up again. Things tend to work in cycles. Sometimes they're in fashion, sometimes they're not. Appraisal systems are an example of this. If you just wait for the cycle to come round you will get our chance again.

Tom Nell also understands that you sometimes have to wait:

> If the issue is large enough it can take three or four years before you get a second chance to get your proposal accepted. Take, for example, losing a new bit of business to another function. Once the company has made this decision they won't change their minds overnight. You may have to wait for years so put it behind you and get on with the job in hand.

When you find yourself in this position it is essential that you lose gracefully, or else you may not be given that second chance. Your immediate concerns should be as follows.

- How can I learn from this defeat?
- How can I help my team to cope with their disappointment?
- How can I best manage the implementation of a decision I did not agree with?

IMPLEMENTING THE UNWANTED DECISION

The worst thing a manager can do when faced with defeat is to go back to his or her department and moan about the stupidity of the decision. This will only make you look powerless, stupid and unstatesmanlike in your subordinates' eyes. True, a team needs a leader who is a powerful advocate with the outside world to fight for their interests. But they can't expect you to win all your battles. If you are concerned with developing *their* political maturity, you should make sure that they understand that you won't win every time. They will look to you as a role model and learn from the way you cope with failure. If you rant and rave about the stupidity of senior management, you will undermine their confidence in the company and also undermine their confidence in you.

When you have failed you've got to support the decision even if it is against you. Remember, if you are tempted to have another go when the decision is final, it begins to look like disloyalty if you are not careful.

Your boss won't appreciate the fact that you are exerting energy in pointlessly arguing with her, instead of implementing the decision.

You've got to fight for what you believe in, but if you've had a fair hearing and the answer is 'no', then you've got to accept it. You need the greatest strength as a manager to support a decision you don't agree with. Don't keep sniping against your boss for saying 'no'. You may think you're undermining her but you're actually undermining yourself. It takes a strong person to support a decision he didn't want.

Don't forget that you aren't the only person who is going to be disappointed. The chances are that your team has been behind you and is also hoping for victory. They may have done a lot of work to help you prepare your proposal. You must think about how to help them to cope with the disappointment and to implement something that they know that you fought against. Try to manage failure positively for the sake of your team. Explain to them why the company has made the decision. This maintains your leadership position. Try to position the argument in the wider business context.

So accepting failure and supporting the decision strengthens your power as a leader. You don't necessarily lose power when you fail, unless you take your defeat badly. Complete the questionnaire below in order to build a picture of how political you are at handling failure.

HOW DO YOU COPE WITH FAILURE?

A. Negative reactions

Do you:	Often	Sometimes	Never
• feel like a failure?			
• take it personally?			
• feel inclined to play it safe and not risk failure in the future?			
• get very angry with the decision-makers?			
• burn your bridges?			
• carry on arguing after a firm 'no'?			
• push and confront so that people dig their heels in?			
• rant and rave to your team about the stupidity of the decision?			
• fail to support the unwanted decision?			

If you answer 'often' or 'sometimes' to a high proportion of the questions in section A, you are in danger of letting your failures undermine your power by handling them badly.

B. Positive reactions

Do you:	Often	Sometimes	Never
• see failure as an inevitable part of a manager's life?			
• try to learn from your failures?			
• make contingency plans in case you fail?			
• Try to understand why the answer was 'no'?			
• maintain good relationships with the people who made the decision?			
• express your disappointment assertively?			
• use your network to find out why you lost?			
• maintain your allies so that you can win in the future?			
• withdraw so that you can rethink and try later?			
• face up to failure and try to turn it around into success in the future?			
• help your team to cope with their disappointment?			
• support the decision once it's fairly made?			
• explain to your team why the business made that decision?			
• maintain your leadership position in the face of defeat?			

If you answer 'often' or 'sometimes' to a fair number of the questions in section B, then you are well on your way to maintaining your power and influence through the way you cope with failure.

If you got a high score on section A and a low score on section B, then you are letting your emotions interfere with your ability to be strategic. People do feel passionately about their jobs and about the projects they are involved with. It is therefore very natural for them to lose their tempers and their objectivity when they suffer defeat. It is easy to feel rejected, threatened or put down if you fail to get the answer you want. But, although passion and anger can be good, they can be destructive if they are not directed into productive channels. Take another look at some of these strategies the next time you lose a battle. Losing gracefully is an important part of the struggle to be successful.

CHAPTER 11

DEVELOPING A POWERFUL IMAGE

Do you *look* like a leader? You will stand a better chance of becoming one if you do. People respond to status and power; they pay more attention to you if they think you have it. We signal our power in many ways: with titles, secretaries, cars, etc. But the main signals that people interpret, often unconsciously, are the signals of status we give out through our dress, grooming and bearing.

Managers, especially the male variety, are uncomfortable with this subject. The managers I interviewed were, in many cases, reluctant to say a lot about how they managed their image. It seems such a shallow, superficial thing to be thinking about. Yet it is so important. Through your image you can either attract or repel. You can make people want to associate with you, feel you are one of them or consider you approachable. On the other hand, you can put up barriers, appear cold and formal, or look inconsequential, low status and frumpy. If such a range of impressions can be the consequence of the way you behave and dress, then it must be worth spending some time thinking about your image.

Even though many of the managers I interviewed had little to say on this subject, they did, none the less, manage their images well. They all looked high status. Their clothes varied in the degree of formality and trendiness, but they were all well dressed and well groomed. They held themselves with a relaxed confidence. Their status showed through small things like watches, quality of shoes and the fact that none of them wore white socks! Although their image is not what gave them their power, it was part of the package, and an important back-up. Without a powerful image you have to work so much harder to be taken seriously.

CONFORM BUT DON'T CREEP

Here is some sound advice on conforming without being boring. 'It's all about paying attention to organisational norms. You shouldn't be overtly rebellious in your appearance, but watch you don't err on the side of being boring.' If you are totally conventional and proper, people won't be attracted to you as a person they want to spend time with. It's dangerous to be seen as a faceless person, a super creep. If you *have* to be that conventional, then you may give the impression that you are a follower rather than a leader. You do need to add something to the conventional image which is uniquely you, something which shows you to be human rather than a company robot. Mike Dearden says, 'If you decide to be flamboyant, to express your personality, you must do so within bounds. Under a previous MD (a Scottish accountant and lawyer), no one here would ever wear brown shoes, they were very much frowned on.' Keith Manning says: 'Don't wear beards, because some people don't like them. By the same token, avoid being too loud. Good grooming is important. Aim to blend in with the wallpaper without disappearing.'

Try to dress in a way that signals your status or, if you haven't much status yet, dress in a way that signals that you are someone on the way somewhere. When I took my first job as a management consultant I decided to wear expensive, good quality clothes. Even though all the other women in the company were secretaries, no one assumed that I was. I was told a few months later that people realised by the way I dressed that I was a consultant, even though I was a woman.

Rosie Harris also thinks that it is important to develop a high-status image.

> Make sure you do high-profile jobs that are seen as critical to what the company is about. *Always* look smart. Invest in good quality clothes and shoes. When I first joined the Prudential most of the women here did not wear suits. I always did (a habit I had formed as an auditor at Deloittes). Junior women began to copy me and wear suits. Another thing which helps to build your image as a leader is to stay late and support your staff when they are working late. Never lose your temper in public. If you have to dress someone down, do it in private. Sometimes, when I am in a hurry, I run. I am told that it gives me a dynamic image.

Physical presence, bearing and size all contribute towards your image. Do you feel, when you walk into a room, that heads are going to turn? You've got to dress relevantly, in clothes that are smart and contemporary, but orthodox. Creative people can be less formal, but not scruffy. A good way to build your image is to stand up at conferences and position yourself as an authority on a particular subject.

You may think that it is unfair that size gives status, as it is something over which we have no control. However, size only gives status if you have good bearing. I see tall people who stoop, and their height doesn't work for them at all. Size helps because big people are more easily noticed. If you are short you just have to get noticed because of other things. Small people with straight backs and confident eyes can make just as much impact.

HAVING A SMART IMAGE BUILDS YOUR CONFIDENCE

One of the most important reasons for keeping up appearances is that you feel better about yourself if you know you look smart and capable. You should be seen as confident, capable and in control. There should be no surprises. You need a good back-up. Image is not just about physical appearance and dress. Your papers should be well produced, properly photocopied or printed and correctly collated. People want to see you as a leader able to cope with anything.

KEEP AN EYE ON CHANGES IN FASHION

Tom Nell is aware of how the game is played:

> Developing a powerful image is about conforming to patterns of behaviour. Fashions emerge among senior managers, like hankies in suit pockets and fob watches. Take an example I heard of. 'One of the senior managers in a company had a health problem for a while and during this time his chauffeur used to carry his briefcase into meetings for him. Very soon, about twenty other managers (none of whom was ill) were to be seen marching into meetings, closely followed by their chauffeurs bearing their briefcases. A lot of us conform without realising we're doing it. It's a way of showing that you've arrived.'
>
> Whitbread is a very sociable company. One way of showing that you belong is to enjoy having a pint with your workmates (even if you don't really enjoy it). If you don't conform to these accepted patterns you may

stick out like a sore thumb. You've got to observe how things are done around here if you want to conform.

If you're alert, you can cotton on to new themes – spot them early, act on them and talk about them before everyone else starts to do so. This is a good example. About ten years ago Whitbread decided that they wanted to get closer to the community. Some managers spotted this as a winning theme and started doing things which conformed to this new trend. As a result they achieved an added amount of influence.

I spotted a new theme in the press, which was writing about liaison between industry and schools. I was enthused by the concept and I began to give talks to schoolkids about life in industry (which was something that I believed we should be doing anyway). Suddenly, a main board subcommittee asked me to make a presentation on the subject. This helped the company and I believe it helped me as well.

Be approachable but not one of the lads

'Although you should get close to your subordinates,' says Keith Manning, 'getting drunk with them or being one of the lads is a mistake. Keep just a little distance. Never come back into the office drunk. Anything that takes away the façade is to be avoided. But at the same time you need to be approachable. I invite anyone to come into my office and talk to me when they want to.'

There is a delicate balance between putting people off with your formality and avoiding loss of status by becoming one of the lads. In Keith Manning's case the trappings of power could intimidate junior people from taking up his invitation to come and talk to him anytime. To get to his office you have to go to the top of the building and walk down a long corridor between beautifully panelled walls, with a thick carpet on the floor. Then you have to get through his secretary who manages Keith's busy diary in a pleasant but firm way. That invitation to 'come and talk to me anytime' needs to be backed up by genuine warmth, and by Keith doing some of the visiting. I am sure this happens in his case because he is a very popular manager. But it's easy to see how a powerful image can both give you status *and* build barriers. Once you become powerful and confident it's easy to forget the fears and hesitations suffered by people lower down the hierarchy. It's no good telling them not to be so foolish, you've got to put yourself out to help them to approach you.

As Tony Hughes says, 'Remove the management cloak. Listen to your employees' ideas.' Tony makes a big effort to go and talk to his employees. He realises that it's up to him to break the barriers.

Jerry Stockbridge's point of view is that you need to let go of some of your status, in order to make yourself human and approachable, but you can't do that if you don't have status in the first place!

> I wear smart suits for important meetings. You only get one chance to make a first impression. When I am addressing a conference I take it seriously and that creates a certain tension. It's good to break this tension with some daffy joke. I use humour to break the ice. You have to have status to be able to let go of it and crack jokes. I'm a naturally shy person. I would rather hide in a corner than get all dressed up and make a presentation. But it's all part of the job.

BE TRUE TO YOURSELF

It's no good trying to develop a powerful image in a way that doesn't fit in with your personality. If people see you as trying to be something that you're not, they will regard you as a follower, rather than as a leader. People are much better at doing things that come naturally, rather than acting a part. Michael Lainas had this experience to relate:

> When I joined Dixons as a director I decided that I should start from a more formal position. I got all the employees together in the canteen at 8.30 am and made an introductory speech. This formality lasted for three days, then I reverted to type. I find it much more natural to be a team-building sort of manager. I do believe that you have to take a flexible approach to your management style.
>
> It is important to recognise that you have got to be forceful when it's needed. You've got to be seen to be firm, even though you have a friendly approach. You've got to be authoritative. Team building implies participation, but you've got to make your own decisions sometimes. As a result of searching for this balance between friendliness and firmness people in powerful positions can seem inconsistent. In spite of this apparent inconsistency people have got to know what are your core values and beliefs.

POWER DRESSING FOR MEN

For obvious reasons, much of the advice on power dressing is different for men and women. I'll start with the men. The question here is not just how to look smart and well groomed, but how to look powerful. Generally, use your clothes to underwhelm. If you want to look powerful you can't break too many rules in the dress code. If you want to stand out then it's better to do so by having well-cut clothes, beautiful ties and flattering colours. Don't try to stand out by being loud or eccentric. Your status will fall away at once.

Shirts

To wear a white shirt with a dark suit is the most formal and the most powerful way you can dress. If you want to appear more friendly and approachable wear light blue shirts and slightly lighter suits. White shirts always look right at night. If you wear striped shirts, remember that the wider the stripe, the more informal you look. Avoid having more than three colours in a shirt. The cuff should show under the coat sleeve, and should be around 5in from the top of the thumb. Shirts should always look clean and well ironed.

Suits

Your suit is the most important and expensive part of your wardrobe, so take care when you choose it. Your suits (and your shirts) should have no more than 35 per cent polyester. Inexpensive suits may look good when you try them on in the shop, but if they look very crushed by lunchtime, then you aren't doing yourself a favour. It's better to have two or three good suits than a whole wardrobe full of crushables! To keep your suit looking good, shake it out at night, and then let it hang freely for half an hour. It's better to wear a suit every other day if you can because that gives it a chance to recover from a day's wear. If you wear pin-striped suits, stripes of ¼in width give the most authority. Wider stripes are less formal. A double-breasted jacket gives a more closed up, less approachable image. A single-breasted jacket is slightly more informal. The most powerful colour for a suit is dark grey, or navy blue with a hint of smoke. Light colours and browns just don't give the same status.

Trousers

Trousers should break on the shoes. The back of the trouser leg should be ½in longer than the front, but turnups should be parallel. Belt buckles should not be too large. Keep an eye on your trouser seats and knees. Nothing makes a manager look more scruffy and unimpressive than to wear suits that are shiny with age, with the wear showing at the knees and seat.

You also detract from your credibility by wearing clothes that are out of fashion. If baggy clothes are in fashion, a tight-fitting suit will look distinctly unfashionable. Avoid wearing clothes that you have grown out of. Nothing looks worse than a plump man in tight trousers! Either cut down on those business lunches or splash out on some new clothes.

Ties

Stripes on ties really work; they give you authority. The stripes should not be more than ½in apart. A thin, red stripe adds authority and a small pattern on the tie can look elegant. Avoid wearing a navy blue tie with a navy suit. The greater the contrast between the tie and the suit, the more powerful you look, and the fewer the colours, the more powerful the tie. Take the smallest colour in the tie and repeat it in your pocket handkerchief. Avoid club ties and large prints. The knot on the tie should fit the collar space and the tie should come down to your belt buckle.

Ties are very useful because you can change them to vary the message you give to the world. There is the sincere tie (narrow stripes of course) that you use for interviews and presentations. Then there is the human tie that you use for staff meetings and creating informality. It may be worth keeping a few spares in your desk drawer so that you can change to fit the occasion. Career women change their accessories to achieve variations in formality; there is no reason why men shouldn't do this too.

Spectacles

These should be as wide as your face and positioned so that you can look through the middle of the lens. They should have a shape which is different to the shape of your face. Square glasses with thick rims denote power. The upper rim of your glasses should be on your eyebrow.

Shoes

Look after your shoes, keep them polished and have at least two pairs so that you can give them a rest after a day of wear. This is especially helpful if you get them wet. It's worth investing in good shoes, because they help your image a lot. Good shoes last much longer anyway, so you may end up spending less in the long run. Always wear black shoes, as brown shoes just don't look right. Never wear white socks. People will write you off if you do. In fact, avoid light coloured socks altogether. People's eyes go to light or bright areas, and you don't want them staring at your feet!

Hair

Your hair needs to be well cut with a definite style. It doesn't matter whether it's curly or straight, short or long (although you need to pay attention to fashion), or whether you have a lot or only a little. The main thing is to have it well groomed.

Beards are a problem. For some reason they are frowned upon in most traditional settings. People with beards are suspected of being alternative and mysterious, perhaps slightly rebellious. Moustaches are less of a problem, but are still seen as not quite mainstream! If you want to be absolutely sure that you've got it right, then a clean-shaven face is safest.

Image consultants

If all of this seems very complicated, try asking your company to send you to an image consultant. See the Useful Addresses section at the back of this book. Image consultants now work with men as much as they work with women, and with impressive results.

POWER DRESSING FOR WOMEN

Much of the general advice for men also applies to women. Dark colours, smart, tailored clothes, good grooming and high quality accessories add several levels to your status. But when it comes to the detail, women have more leeway. This is both an advantage and a problem, since it also means women can make more mistakes!

Get the detail right

Women managers have learnt that they need to wear suits or tailored dresses to give the right image, but they sometimes err with the detail. Their feet and legs sometimes give them away. It's hard to keep high-heeled shoes in good condition, but it is worth the effort. If I see a woman with torn heels or scuffed shoes I assume automatically that she isn't high status. Shoes should also be darker than the hemline, and should always be filled with stockinged legs, even in hot weather! Umbrellas, handbags, jewellery, indeed all accessories, need to give a consistent image – good quality, flattering colours, but never too loud. Handbags for power dressing should be firm rather than floppy. Floppy handbags are only for casual outfits. Large, chunky earrings are in fashion now, and they do a lot to make a severe and formal outfit look feminine and attractive. But large, dangly earrings are also in fashion. They never work because they overemphasise the fact that you are a woman and focus attention on your sexuality rather than on your status. Hair needs to be well styled. Severe haircuts, unless they suit you very well, can make you look too macho. Long hair is normally more feminine and flattering, but it does need to be kept in order. Your power suit will fail to give you status if you have a wild, unruly head of unkempt hair.

Rosie Faunch thinks that her appearance is important at work.

If my hair needs cutting I don't feel good about myself. I usually wear suits, clothes that look competent but not aggressive. I also want to look approachable. I wear a navy suit when I want to look my most trustworthy and conventional. Dresses are certainly more feminine. I have noticed that I get treated more gently when I am wearing a dress, although this is not 100 per cent reliable! I also think that it is important to keep up with fashion, but in a subtle way.

Colour

Another problem for powerful women is how to use colour. Dark colours look just as good and just as high status on a woman as on a man. But don't err on the side of looking too drab or too severe. Use blouses in flattering shades, or jewellery and scarves, to soften the image, and to make you stand out without being loud. Women have a great advantage in that they have more leeway with styles and colour, and can use them to flatter their figures and stand out among rows of drab men. But it needs skill and knowledge to use this to advantage. Colour analysts can be of great help here. They can help you to choose colours and styles that flatter, and plan your wardrobe so that you minimise spending on clothes.

Make-up

Make-up is another detail that can help you to look well finished and groomed. If you make up in shades that suit your skin tones then you create an effect that looks subtly good, without looking overdone. Glittery eyeshadow, false eyelashes and very bright lipstick are all overdoing it. Managing your image is not about trying to be something you're not. It's about being aware of your strengths and using your clothes and make-up to make the best of them. If you look good, you automatically look wiser, more credible and more experienced.

LESS TRADITIONAL ORGANISATIONS

Smart, fashionable, tailored clothes are not appropriate in all organisations. In the creative world of advertising, marketing, PR, sales promotion, etc, it is sometimes more appropriate to wear clothes that are casual, colourful and trendy. In parts of the civil service, the academic world and the scientific world it seems to be fashionable to be as unfashionable as possible! By all means fit in with your environment and don't offend norms. But remember this. However casual, trendy or sober you need to look, it never pays to look scruffy, dowdy or dirty! The really powerful, high-status people in any of these environments don't usually wear dirty shirts or worn and shiny trousers.

PEOPLE WHO BREAK THE RULES

There are people who break the rules and none the less manage to be very powerful indeed. If you think that you have so many advantages and so much charisma that you can break even the most basic of rules and still be looked up to, then that's fine. Most of us haven't such a head start, however, so we do need to get our clothes to work for us.

BODY LANGUAGE

Body language is very important in denoting status; it reinforces the message given by your power suit that you are someone to be taken seriously. Chapter 9 shows you how to use body language to be assertive. Here are a few tips on strengthening your body language in order to look powerful.

Bearing is the most significant signaller of status. A straight back, a confident posture and a clear, steady, unafraid gaze will always deliver the message that you are powerful. Use gestures that denote strength, and which are unhesitant and decisive. Vigorous head nodding or an averted gaze, fidgeting, twisting a ring – these are all examples of mannerisms that detract from our power by saying that we are not entirely in control. When you want to look powerful, keep still, look alert and use only firm gestures. Don't let your body language give you away, for then your power suit will look like fancy dress rather than the real thing!

When you walk into a room, stride in purposefully and look genuinely interested in meeting whoever is in there. When you sit, remember to keep your back up straight. Far too many people let their status fade when they slouch into a chair.

If you want to be the sort of powerful senior manager who is also human and approachable, then you can use your body language to convey this message. Avoid a rigid posture and an unsmiling face; a severe look always puts barriers between you and other people. An unsmiling face does *not* help your image, it makes you seem unapproachable to people below you, and fearful or out of your depth to people above you. Don't throw away your status to become one of the lads, because they won't respect you. Keep your high-status poise and mannerisms, but use smiles, open gestures and encouraging words to soften your power image.

Here is a questionnaire which will help you to check whether your clothes and behaviour are working for you to reinforce your power.

IMAGE CHECK

	Yes	No
Do you know what is in fashion?		
Do you have friends who can tell you?		
Do you conform (within reason) to accepted management behaviour?		
Are you up to date on current themes?		
Do you avoid being boring and overconventional?		
Do you avoid things that make you stand out too much? (Beards and earrings for men, dangly earrings and low cleavages for women)		
Are you well groomed? Is your hair well cut, are your fingernails clean, etc?		
Do you keep your dignity in public – avoid shouting, fighting, getting drunk, etc?		
Are you firm and forceful when you need to be?		
Do you make yourself approachable without losing status?		
Do you sometimes wear white shirts (or blouses) when you need to look formal?		
Are your shirts (or blouses) always clean and well ironed?		
Are your suits dark, well cut and not out of date?		
Do your suits still look uncrushed at the end of the day?		
Do you avoid wearing white or light-coloured socks?		
Are your stripes close enough to denote status?		
Do your clothes fit you well?		
Do you avoid large prints and loud colours?		
Are your accessories (shoes, briefcases, handbags) real leather, good quality and cared for?		
Is your jewellery fashionable but discreet?		
Do you wear colours that suit you?		

If you're able to answer 'yes' to most of these questions, then your image is helping you to reinforce your power and status. If you answered 'no' to one-quarter or more of the questions, then you still have some work to do. When you do get around to working on your image you will be pleasantly surprised by the favourable reaction you will get from other people. They may not notice the detailed changes, but they will respond to the overall impression of status, and you will find it easier to influence them.

CHAPTER 12

INFLUENCING OTHER DEPARTMENTS

LATERAL COMMUNICATIONS

Mintzberg established that managers spend between 50 and 90 per cent of their time talking with other people at work. Ten per cent of this time is spent talking to bosses, 40 per cent talking to subordinates and 50 per cent talking to people outside of their chain of command.[10] This chapter is about the last 50 per cent, the time that managers spend in what we call 'lateral communications', talking with and influencing people outside of their departments, over whom they have no authority. This is often the most unpredictable, risky and frustrating part of a manager's job. All too often managers talk to other managers without really communicating. Yet, without being good at 'lateral' relations, a manager cannot get the co-operation and resources he or she needs to do their job properly.

Naïve managers see this part of their job as either unnecessary or simply as office politics (which they wouldn't indulge in if they had the choice). These managers grudge the time spent on co-ordinating with and influencing other managers. They fail to understand the pressures and clashes of interests and values that make these lateral relations awkward and demanding on their time and patience.

It's very tempting, having failed to get co-operation from a pressurised fellow manager, to go back to your boss and say, 'You gave me an impossible task! How can I complete the project if Fred refuses to play ball and the project depends on the participation of his department?' Your boss, who has a different perspective from you, is not very likely to blame Fred for not playing ball and take sides with you. He or she is much more likely to see your failure to get Fred to participate as a failure on your part to get the project off the ground. You will be judged on your ability to work with other managers (including difficult ones) just as much as you will be judged on your technical capacity and your ability to manage your own team. How could he or she judge you otherwise? Companies specialise functions and put them in separate departments. No one manager can provide all the expertise needed, you have to co-ordinate with other functions to get things done. You cannot just do your own job and ignore other departments – you need each other, you must work together for the organisation to function.

It is very understandable if you do sometimes find it difficult to influence other departments. There are many reasons why these difficulties exist. But they must be understood and dealt with if you are to manage effectively. All the managers I interviewed experienced some difficulties in this area, but they had each worked out a series of strategies for overcoming problems. They regarded the time spent on building lateral relations as necessary and not wasted.

The cost of not devoting time to lateral relations

There is no doubt that influencing other departments takes time. All of the success stories in this chapter are about managers spending a lot of time cultivating their colleagues in other departments, understanding their points of view, explaining, negotiating and doing favours. You need to spend at least 10 per cent of your time on developing good lateral relations. To a manager who wants to focus on performance, who just wants to do his or her job, this will seem like an unacceptable expenditure of time. Yet if you don't devote enough time to lateral relations, you will waste much more than 10 per cent of your time fighting with other departments, banging your head against brick walls and just not getting things done.

In many research studies middle managers are reported to complain that inter-group conflict is seldom dealt with in their companies and that, even when it is, attempts are inadequate. Many state that the most important unsolved problem of their organisation is inter-group rivalry, lack of co-operation and poor communication. They speak of the dog-eat-dog communication problems that exist between middle managers.[11]

If you fail to manage your own lateral relations so that you avoid these communication problems things can only get worse:

- conflicts will harden and perpetuate themselves;

- information will be distorted;
- hostility and suspicion will grow;
- stereotyping will build even larger barriers;
- individual and group energies will be spent in gossip, tactics and conflict, when they could have been spent in collaboration.

Even if all of this is going on around you, you can break the cycle by getting to know people from other departments, trying to understand them, and doing favours for them. Try to avoid head-on confrontation. Get to know key people, and be nice to them. If everyone else is in conflict they will appreciate someone who isn't. Don't join in the fray and help to perpetuate inter-group conflict. Friends that you make in other departments will be useful allies to you on your way to the top. Don't spend your time making enemies out of them instead.

DEALING WITH PEOPLE YOU DON'T SEE EVERY DAY

As long as individuals are dealing with each other regularly, they usually evolve easy and simple methods of sorting things out. There will be occasional personality conflicts, but these are not normally tolerated for long within a busy team. Within a working team people usually adopt comfortable routines of give and take to exchange ideas and help each other.[4]

When people only deal with each other infrequently and belong to different departments, then it gets much more difficult. Your irregular contact means that you can't develop an easy and predictable way of interacting. And teams tend to develop unity by stereotyping outsiders. This puts a further barrier between you and your counterpart from across the corridor. All of this means that you must explain and expound in lengthy and often discomforting detail. People who don't develop the skills and patience to do this will undoubtedly have frustrating and irritating experiences with colleagues from other departments.[4]

Tom Nell, as a member of the finance department, is always dealing with other departments:

> I had to learn about this the hard way. Our relations were particularly problematic with the service departments. My approach is to try to establish what is going to be mutually beneficial and to generate a spirit of 'Let's work on this together.'

It is easy to see the finance department as people who ask difficult questions and who don't understand the business well enough. They can feel very isolated and detached as part of the finance team and then act that way. This just reinforces the stereotype. Eventually I found a way of reducing this problem. When dealing with a service department I would make the representative from that department become a member of our functional team. They would still be working for their own department, but I would ensure that they felt that they belonged to our team. For each business task we would share our initial thoughts on the way to tackle that task. In the end, we would develop together an approach that the finance department could say 'yes' to. We reinforced the team membership thing by taking the service department person out for drinks with us.

Tom found this to be an effective way of breaking down the harmful stereotyping and isolation. When you develop your ideas first and then present them to the other department, you have all the barriers and stereotypes to overcome. Working together from the early stages of a task does solve a lot of these problems, although, if the representative from the outside department becomes too integrated into your team he or she may have to overcome barriers when going back with the joint proposal to his or her own team!

If you are a financial person, you know that the danger is that you will be seen as negative and threatening by other departments. You've got to know what you're trying to sell other departments, what you have to offer that will make their job easier. Try to be seen as the person who can help them to manage their resources, not as the person who is always saying, 'You can't do that!' Treat people as you would like to be treated yourself.

DIFFERENCES IN GOALS AND VALUES

There are often differences in ideas about how work is to be done as it crosses departmental boundaries. Different groups usually have different priorities and pressures. Take the classic differences between sales and production. Sales are naturally concerned with customer satisfaction, while production are concerned with optimum schedules and economic runs or batches. Sales often make unrealistic promises to customers that production can only fulfil if they are unprofitable. Tight deadlines or special requirements to fit a customer's unique needs may involve production in uneconomic short runs, unscheduled overtime or disruption of work in the factory. Production will resist and involve sales in embarrassing renegotiations with the customer.[4]

If you don't understand the pressures faced by your colleagues from other departments you may find yourself fighting battles with them that neither side will win. It is all too common that people from one department haven't the faintest idea what goes on in another. When consulting at a brewery some years ago, I discovered that warfare between production and marketing was caused by just such ignorance. The advertising people were always complaining that when they created a demand for a product through a successful campaign, the brewery let them down by having insufficient beer to meet the demand. What the marketing department didn't know was that the brewery needed a lead time of four weeks to produce the extra quantities. A simple exchange of information solved an age-old problem.

Don't let ignorance of this sort damage your interdepartmental relations. Stay in touch with other departments. Mike Dearden says that he spends up to 10 per cent of his time keeping in touch with his colleagues in other departments, and that this time is fruitfully spent.

> You've got to know the influences in other departments, then you can negotiate with them – do a trade. You trade with them by building up favours. Sometimes I store up a favour I know I can do for someone and then do a trade when I need something.
>
> When I want to get something accepted I pre-sell as much as possible. I get around the key commentators and talk to them about it. I go through my proposal, draw objections and get their input. Once I withdrew a project because I saw that it was unacceptable. The personal touch helps. It's best to ask someone face to face. It's more fruitful than memos or telephone calls. It's also best to go to *their* office. Most people are happier to receive you in their office, you'll get a more sympathetic reaction there.

Tony Hughes agrees that you need to talk things over face to face.

> I am a disruptive force in an office. I don't like paper, it's all about talking to each other as far as I am concerned. Paper is about covering your arse, I think you should talk instead. Build up a network by talking to everyone, eyeball to eyeball. You will have much better odds on succeeding. It is better to confront things positively, issues, not people.

Another classic problem between departments is the difference of perspective between people in staff and line jobs. As Michael Lainas says,

> When you are in a staff role you have to accept that people in operational roles feel they are under more pressure. When you are in a staff role you must ask yourself what is it that you're trying to achieve for other departments. You've got to look for mutual co-operation, 'What do they want from me, and what do I want from them?' Too often managers in staff jobs become unco-operative in an effort to reduce pressures on their department, forgetting that their function is to support other managers. Impossible requests do need to be toned down, but in a spirit of co-operation, by asking, 'How can we work out a way to give you the essentials, in line with our other commitments?'

DIFFERING PHILOSOPHIES

It is not uncommon that people in other departments will have different philosophies, approaches to work and even standards. This can put up a significant block to good interdepartmental relations, as Keith Manning found:

> I had a problem with a senior director of Bull HN. He was the most senior of the people who report to the managing director, and had a lot of power. My problem was that I was supposed to be determining strategy but couldn't get through to him. Strategies are pointless if one of the implementers doesn't believe in them. There was a history of conflict between us which did not help, but the real problem was our difference in philosophy. He didn't believe in strategy, he thought it was for the birds. Being tied within a framework gave him real problems. When I went to him with a proposal that he didn't like I got a bad-tempered tirade.
>
> First of all I had to decide that I wasn't afraid of him, that he wasn't a threat to me. I decided that it wasn't a question of winning personally, that I could cope with losing my job if it came to that. You begin to make progress when you're confident enough to take what you consider to be correct action, regardless of personal consequences. My practical solution to this communication problem was in two parts. As I couldn't get through to this director I needed to win the arguments in open meetings, so I spoke to the other directors and won their support. I also spoke to his subordinates to influence them and find out what was going on. I could

get them to do small things to co-operate with my department without going through him, but of course that did not suffice for the real issues.

In this case, the problem was over the approach to strategy, whether thinking should be short term or long term. This is just one of a number of differences that can block good working relations between departments. People in the marketing department are often seen as superficial in their thinking, research may be seen as nit-picking, slow and unresponsive to the customer, and personnel may be seen as too soft and left-wing. When negotiations break down for these reasons, highly political conflicts arise. These conflicts are often much more time-consuming than the effort spent on getting to know people and resolve differences *before* they block communication.

INFLUENCE THROUGH NEGOTIATION

When there is no obvious answer, no obvious decision that can resolve a difference of interest between departments, and there is no way forward except through warfare or negotiation then, obviously, negotiation is best.

A typical problem arises when your boss demands that you do a task which requires help or resources from another department. If they respond with serious delays or a refusal then you cannot meet your deadline. Managers often react to this situation with indignation or outrage. They shoot from the hip in ways that are counterproductive:

- they try to bully or pressurise their colleague into submission;
- they accuse their colleague of not having the company's interest at heart, or of being inefficient or incompetent;
- they mistakenly assume that it is just a misunderstanding or a communication problem, and that when the situation is clarified, co-operation will be forthcoming;
- they assume that there must be a clever way of fooling the other party and overcoming their resistance.[+]

Bullying, threatening and criticising are all likely to make the situation worse, rather than better. Assuming that it is a communication problem can also be a formula for not finding a solution. This assumption is based on the naïve belief that the organisation is one big family and that everyone has the same interests and goals. This is simply not so. It is common for other departments to have different interests and to get rewarded for doing things that may not be consistent with your immediate needs in completing your task. Many conflicts over what should be done are not simply misunderstandings, they are often real conflicts over goals and tactics. The plan to 'fool' the other department into co-operating depends on the people concerned being fairly stupid and having short memories. Usually the opposite is true. It is a dangerous strategy because it assumes that you will never have to work with that department again. The chances are that you will, and people will remember that you aren't to be trusted.

In the end, you often have no choice but to negotiate. Clarify your needs and make sure you understand the other person's constraints. Then, if you can, modify your request to fit in with their constraints. If you've built up credibility over the years by taking the trouble to get to know people, and by demonstrating flexibility, the other side is likely to show some flexibility too.

Negotiations are time-consuming and can be destroyed by emotional blame-fixing or threats. Negotiations assume that both parties want to build or continue a relationship, not just solve the immediate problem.

Most people will put requests from other departments to the bottom of the pile. You've got to chase it up, and deal with the other person directly. You've got to show them why it is in their interests and also get them to see how important it is to you. If, for example, they are going to give you some information, you could offer to summarise it for them so that they can put it to use for themselves. If you are doing a survey which involves them in producing material, offer to show them the results.

Most people don't do things because they simply fail to get round to doing them. The delay can cause you a problem with your deadlines. If you cultivate relationships over a period of time it will be easier to influence people to give you their help when you need it. I work through an unexpressed system of favours. There is an open exchange of favours which always operates. You have to use it extensively to be successful. You've got to find out what people are interested in and what they need, and give it where possible. Favours will stop if you stop giving them. Roger French tells the following story:

> When Deloittes merged with Coopers in the UK, I found that I had suddenly lost a large part of my old network since firms in so many countries chose not to follow the rest of Deloittes in their merger with Coopers. I had joined a completely new network and had to establish new

contacts. In the first month I visited up to twenty operations. There was no direct need for me to do this. In the process I offered help where I could. One department wanted to meet people in the European network so I set that up for them. I was able to give another country help in a particular marketing situation. I never said, if I help you will you do something for me in exchange? When running the Southern African practices I cultivated the audit partners regularly through informal chats in the office and social occasions. I only asked for favours at a small percentage of these meetings. In Germany the culture is different. Although they do invite you to social occasions, when they meet you in the office they expect you to do business.

When you do go to see someone to ask for help, it is important to present confidently, with the assumption that you are going to get what you want. Use your charm. The quality of the request is important. Often people don't respond as you want them to because of unclear communication. You have got to tell them:

- exactly what you want;
- when you need it by;
- how accurate it needs to be;
- how detailed; and
- whether you can pay for it or expect it for nothing.

Roger finds that as long as he keeps cultivating relationships, and his requests are reasonable and clearly presented, he will succeed in influencing his colleagues in other departments. Unreasonable requests don't get much sympathy – like the request from the corporate planning department for a five-year plan from a plant manager whose factory had had a fire the day before!

When negotiations fail – move up the hierarchy

If negotiations with the managers at your level fail, then you may have to escalate things by going up the hierarchy. Jerry Stockbridge explains how he puts on the pressure when people are reluctant to co-operate.

I find that conflicts over resources sometimes arise with technical departments or computer departments. A typical situation is something like this: I want them to do design or development work and they say they're short of staff and have other priorities. You have no choice, you can't use anyone else, so you've *got* to get them to co-operate.

I usually try to get them to sign some sort of internal contract. I negotiate with them something that they *can* manage, even though they are short staffed. Usually, if I tie it all down with letters it works at that stage, and I don't have to do anything more.

But sometimes, people renege on these agreements. Then you have to escalate it up the hierarchical chain. You say to your opposite number, if you can't resolve it, who can? You find the person up the chain who can resolve it and you talk to him, or get your boss to. If an important contract is at stake the senior person will lean on your opposite number to do what you need him to do.

The point is that Jerry stays cool and works out what he needs to do at each level of difficulty to solve his problem. He has learnt not to let his frustration or impatience lead to rows, nor does he burn any bridges behind him. He tells a story of how he learnt this the hard way:

Managing co-operation between departments is more difficult when you are not senior. Here is an example of a mistake I made when I was much more junior and was responsible for cable planning. The sales department used to take speculative orders for business circuits, then get these orders confirmed by the customer later. But often the orders were modified, or didn't materialise. When this happened the sales department failed to tell us, so we had to plug on with putting more cables in which weren't going to be used.

I didn't like this, so I wrote to the person in charge of sales (who was a level above me in the hierarchy). I proposed a solution to the problem and asked who I could liaise with on his side. But my letter had a phrase in it – *this waste must stop* – which infuriated the sales manager. My boss called me in and told me that the manager was fuming about being confronted by someone more junior. Apparently when he got to the phrase 'this waste must stop', he got so enraged that he never read my proposal for solving the problem. I was asked to rephrase, and to let my boss sort it out, which he did and my proposal was accepted.

Now British Telecom is much more informal. I would have no problem trying to approach someone more senior directly. But I have learnt to be careful about how I approach them. Those ill-chosen words 'this waste must stop' were not the best for opening a dialogue.

MAKE SURE YOU APPROACH THE RIGHT PEOPLE

When you want to influence your colleagues in other departments to back a new project, make sure you get some powerful people on your side. You must accept that you may fail to influence some of them, because of differences in philosophy or values, but if you convince enough sponsors, you may be able to neutralise your opposition.

Tony Hughes has this tale to tell:

> When I was trying to get Whitbread to take on TGI Fridays I made it through the strength of my belief and using this belief to convince my sponsors. On paper it looked like a very costly, risky project so I didn't convince everyone at first. But I did win over two powerful sponsors. These were the person in charge of strategic planning and acquisitions and the chairman of the retail division. Also, my present boss gave me a lot of support. Everyone else resisted, but my sponsors were powerful enough to get things done. Getting sponsors behind you is the most important bit. Judgement of who to approach is vital. You need to seek out people with similar core values to you, because this means it is more likely they will trust you. Although some of my colleagues were very negative about TGI Fridays I won through by choosing the right sponsors. Now the people who were originally seen as 'negative' have become cautious positives!

In summary, make sure that your lateral relations are good by:

- devoting time to it;
- putting yourself in your colleagues' shoes;
- overcoming harmful stereotypes by getting to know people in other departments;
- overcoming resistance to proposals by working with other departments to produce joint solutions;
- understanding the pressures on your colleagues;
- talking things over face to face when possible;
- avoiding threats and bullying;
- negotiating when genuine differences and difficulties block your way;
- moving up the hierarchy when negotiations fail;
- making sure that you approach the right person, the person who has the power to help.

WATCHING OUT FOR DIRTY POLITICS

This book is written for people who want to find a route to influence that doesn't involve them in machiavellian power plays and dirty politics. But it's not enough just to say 'avoid manipulative behaviour'. Power struggles and self-seeking politics are practised in nearly every organisation. If you put your nose in the air, hold up the hem of your skirt and say 'I am going to stay clean and uninvolved', you are putting yourself in danger. This is not an argument for advising that if you can't lick them, join them. But it *is* an argument for becoming alert to what is going on all around you, and finding a way to protect yourself from its effects. If you want to be able to continue to live with yourself, you will want to protect yourself with behaviour that is strategic, but not machiavellian. And that is what this chapter is about.

There is no doubt that if you move up the ladder into jobs which present you with power, you will also come up against risk, and against people who see you as an enemy, at least from time to time. Depending on the culture of your organisation, you will certainly get involved in political battles of one sort or another. The managers I interviewed confirmed this.

'You must accept that politics are an integral part of most businesses,' says Michael Lainas. 'Don't allow yourself to be deluded into thinking that political processes don't exist. You need to identify how to use the political process in a constructive way – with integrity rather than in a subversive and divisive way.'

Rosie Harris agrees that you can't turn a blind eye to politics. 'You can't wipe it [politics] out of an organisation. A lot of manoeuvring goes on. I just keep informed through my network so that I always know what is going on. It helps me to stay well positioned.'

Jerry Stockbridge would prefer to have nothing to do with politics but accepts that it would be unrealistic to ignore it. 'I prefer to shy away from politics. The most difficult thing in most jobs is how to judge politics. It seems like an unhappy choice between spending [too much] time on getting people to like you, *or* spending time on achieving goals. People who achieve goals do tend to be kept on. But you can't really avoid politics, even if you want to. It can prey on your mind and trip you up. I would like to think that I have made a lot of friends in British Telecom. My political philosophy is this: if you don't shit on people on the way up, they'll treat you well on the way down.'

Even someone with a distaste for politics, who would prefer to spend his or her time achieving, should understand the dangers of trying to completely ignore the black art.

EXAMPLES OF DIRTY POLITICS

Dirty politics exists in many forms. Traditional unsavoury political behaviour includes:

- managing information and plans to your advantage;
- being strategic and instrumental in your behaviour;
- seeking approval from above; and
- being cautious in telling the truth.

It's not a bad idea to be aware of the sorts of things people get up to. At the very least, to be forewarned is to be forearmed. It's also worth while making sure that you don't ruin your reputation as an honest broker by becoming involved in any of these ploys.

Creating monopolies to increase power

This is an example of a manipulative strategy that can inflate (usually temporarily) the personal power of a manager. There are several kinds of monopolistic practices. Managers sometimes create a monopoly of information – gaining and holding on to critical knowledge which others must use and therefore depend on them to provide. They may, alternatively, establish a monopoly of the ability to deliver favours, for example, by controlling access to certain kinds of permission or resources. We saw in Chapter 12 how swapping favours can be an effective influence strategy. For example, if one person digs himself into a position where only he can distribute significant favours, then he is hogging this source of influence for himself, and denying it to the others around him.

One way of monopolising favours is to get yourself into a position where no one else apart from you has access to the boss. Anyone who needs something that requires the boss's approval has to go through you. Such people become bottlenecks because they don't like delegating to subordinates, and don't like to allow outsiders to communicate with their people. They are afraid that their subordinates will learn too much about their hard-won techniques and knowledge, so they give or allow little training, insist on doing part of the job themselves and give as little information as possible. They are the 'tell them only what they need to know' variety of managers. In the short term this kind of behaviour can increase their power. Their subordinates don't learn much from them, so they never learn to perform effectively. Even when these managers need to delegate because work is piling up, they can't, because no one else can do the work as well as they can. They have made sure of this. It may make them feel more powerful and as if they are the only person worth their salt, but it also creates enormous pressures when times are busy and work is expanding.

Tactics of this sort usually have their roots in insecurities of some kind. These bosses are not confident enough to tolerate subordinates learning through making mistakes. Nor can they cope with any challenge to their superiority from their people. Some senior managers need always to be seen in a good light. They tend to take the credit for the good things you do, but if you perform badly they write a report saying, 'my man has cocked up'!

Ploys of this sort do the organisation no good. Subordinates aren't developed; information is withheld from those who require it; and needless bottlenecks occur.

Manipulating facts to increase influence

There are managers who will manipulate information, giving part of the truth, but not the whole truth. Many use these tactics to defeat the opposition instead of openly confronting issues. We see this happening often in politics, but it is just as common, though not so publicised, in organisational life. People don't necessarily tell lies, but they give a part of the truth which is damaging to the opposition and withhold anything that sheds a favourable light. Instead of examining their opponents' proposals and building arguments over the issues, they try to discredit their opponents through rumours and through ascribing devious motives to them. They may suggest widespread disillusionment with the opposition, or use scorn and ridicule to turn opinions against them.

Another way of manipulating facts is to present a range of options, but to have one option (your preferred option) clearly standing out above the others, through the way you present. You don't openly advise the selection of your preferred option, you just depend on presenting alternatives in a way that makes it likely that your favourite will be chosen.

Manipulating peoples' emotions

Emotional blackmail is a familiar tactic. People use subtle or sometimes quite crass ways of influencing people through making them feel guilty or sympathetic. Many of us do this without realising it: 'After all the help I gave you on the Phoenix project I can't believe you're going to let me down!' It's a dangerous habit. It can work, in the short term, but people will soon come to despise you for it and you will lose your influence. An alternative to arousing guilt is to arouse fear through threats: 'If you don't agree to do this for me I'll make sure that you find it difficult the next time you ask for a day off.'

Sometimes the threats are open, sometimes they are thinly veiled: 'If you don't take this transfer the board may see you as someone who isn't too interested in promotion.' When people are manoeuvring you to do things that are in their interests, but not in yours, they often resort to using threats or some other sort of manipulation. They also do it without any concern for your safety or your future.

Manipulative negotiation

There is some manipulation of facts and positioning in many negotiations. Having a fall-back position which you don't reveal at the start is a less than open and honest tactic. But at least that is an acceptable part of negotiation, and the chances are that your opposite number has been taught to do the same things. Manipulative negotiation is where withholding tactics are taken to the extreme. Here are some examples.

- Stressing the advantages of your scheme to the other person but minimising the benefits to you. This strategy is designed to make you look unselfish and as if you have the other person's interests at the top of your priorities. It assumes that the other person is naïve. Normally they will be wondering why you are so enthusiastic about the proposition if you have so little to gain. You are more likely to be trusted if you are open about the benefits to you.

- Keeping your own views to yourself and not revealing them until the others have put their cards on the table.
- Threatening sanctions if the other person won't play ball. Bluffing about your power to be a threat if you haven't any.
- Using side issues to distract attention from the main issue when you are not getting your way.
- Constantly questioning the opponent's position when you are under attack.

Manipulative negotiation techniques will erode your influence in the end. Your opponents will respect you if you are a skilled but clean negotiator. Even if you get less than what you wanted in some cases, an honest approach will gain you allies who will help you in the future. Using devious tactics will lose you this long-term advantage.

Being strategic and instrumental in relationships

There are people who will befriend you when they need your support and who will drop you like a hot potato when you are no longer of any use to them. You can usually spot these people a mile off; their insincerity shows. You can tell by the name dropping, the lack of real warmth, the other people who are suddenly out of their favour, just what sort of person they are. When you join a company everybody warns you about the local machiavellian smart alec. They are not as clever as they think they are. They defeat themselves.

Dropping people in it

One way of deviously harming a person is to agree to support them, and then fail to do so. Greg Dyke had this happen to him:

> When I was at TV-am I decided to take on Kerry Packer and confront him. He had just bought into the company, but I felt that we needed to oppose him. I lobbied before the meeting and got the other executives to agree to support me. I stood up, made my attack and nobody else said a word!

Greg obviously survived this débâcle, but he has never forgotten it.

Jim Davies has also been on the receiving end of a let-down by colleagues. Recently, there was a breakaway from Saatchis by a small group of account directors. The breakaways had been running a large and important account for Saatchis:

> When the breakaway happened I went immediately to the client and spoke to them openly about it. I discussed our work with them and agreed to solve the one weakness which the client pointed out. We solved it and the client said, you won't lose any business. However, some time afterwards the client told me that he had decided to take a big brand away from Saatchis and give it to the breakaway group. One of the breakaway account directors and he were very matey. I am using other senior contacts in the client company to try to rescue the account.

UNINTENTIONAL MANIPULATION

The examples I have used so far are of tactics which are premeditated and deliberate. They are mainly indulged in by people who are seeking to look after their own interests, and who don't see the good of the organisation and of their colleagues as a top priority. But it also happens that people who seek safety and approval from their seniors sometimes manage through manipulation, and it is so ingrained that they do not realise that they are doing it. This is not uncommon in strongly traditional, hierarchical organisations where playing it safe and gaining approval from the top are the main motivators. An environment where everyone's attention is mainly focused on how to get promoted encourages closed, manipulative behaviour.

There is a difference between managing through manipulation and managing through control. You control people when you guide their behaviour but let them know you are doing so. Manipulation is trying to control others without them knowing it, and for your ends, not theirs. The managers who use unintentional manipulation would reject the more blatant forms of using other people to their own advantage. But subtle office politics is not normally so clear as outright lying, using and discarding people, or destroying your enemies. For these people being indirect, devious and closed is a way of adapting to a culture that encourages that sort of behaviour. They become manipulative at first because it works, then it becomes a habit that they are not conscious of, and they would be puzzled by it if they could detach themselves and gaze objectively at their own political dramas.

Here are some of the subtle forms of unintentional negative political behaviours. Again I should warn that the short-term advantage of using these methods is outweighed by the longer term destruction of trust and allies.[12]

False supportiveness

You can influence people by using interpersonal skills to make them feel that you are sympathetic, attentive to their needs and aware that they are especially important. If you really feel this way about the other person then you are not being instrumental. But when you win a person's support by deliberately making eye contact, leaning forward attentively, and showing warmth and interest without any genuine feelings, then you are being manipulative in a very sophisticated way.

Name dropping

There is name dropping and there is name dropping. If you set out openly to win powerful sponsors for what you think is a sound proposal, and tell everyone just who is backing you, then you are non-manipulatively using reference power to help you to get your proposal accepted. This is a common and accepted thing to do. Manipulative name droppers don't work like that. They let it be mentioned in passing just how much time they have spent with the 'name', just how much informal contact they have with the 'name' and just how many 'names' they have in their diary or address book. They are trying to let you know that you are up against the big guns. They are trying to influence you by implying that they have the support of these 'names'. They may or may not be bluffing or exaggerating. This device often backfires and makes them appear creepy rather than credible. It has the other disadvantage of being a subtle put-down to the other person who hasn't got such 'names' in his diary.

Saying one thing and meaning another

Saying one thing but giving the message that you mean something different is a most powerful form of manipulation. These are some examples of introductory statements that try to deny what is about to follow.

- I don't mean to interrupt you. (Of course I mean to interrupt you, otherwise why am I doing it?)
- I don't mean to be defensive. (But I am jolly well going to be!)
- I don't want you to be upset about what I am trying to say. (But I know that what I am going to say is pretty upsetting.)
- I don't mean to rationalise my actions (But I'm going to give some good old-fashioned excuses.)

These statements are a manipulative attempt to talk the other person out of their natural response. You are trying to seduce people out of their resentment or anger. They show that you are afraid of being direct and open with other people.

Thank you for the feedback. This is a code for the fact that you hate what you have just been told, it's very upsetting, you hate the giver of the criticism and disagree with them totally. However, you're not going to let on that you're upset and you're not going to get into an argument over it. You would rather let them think that you are big enough to take it, but bide your time, nurture your hurt feelings and get back at them eventually.

We are glad to have you here. This is said by people in the regions who are being visited by people from head office. It is also said to auditors and consultants. What it really means is: 'I think I'm doing pretty well and don't want any help from outsiders. If there are any problems then I would rather solve them on my own, without interference from people who don't know the local business.' This is usually followed by hospitable statements like: 'I hope your journey down was painless', 'I hope your hotel is comfortable', 'How about joining us for lunch/ drinks?', and finally, 'When are you going back?' This is code for: 'There is no real reason for you being here and I find your presence rather threatening. But I am going to put myself over as one of the friendly ones, one of the good guys with nothing to hide or to lose.'

I am just trying to be helpful. This is the flip-side of the coin. This is the greeting from the visitor from head office or the auditor or consultant who is really there to evaluate and report back to top management on areas that need improvement, like your job, for example. He knows he is going to ruffle some feathers and he is feeling pretty defensive about it.

I am offering you a development opportunity. If a development opportunity really *is* being offered then this is not manipulative. But often this is a euphemism for: 'I am not happy with what you are doing and I want to move you somewhere else', or: 'This rather grotty job has come up in Outer Mongolia and nobody else is willing to go there.' This is the most callous and unhelpful of manipulative statements, if done deliberately. Often, however, people fool themselves and instead of facing up to the issues, they talk themselves into believing that they cannot be open about the problem, and that their subordinate *will* gain from having the change.

People are our most important asset. There isn't a company where somebody doesn't trot this out at some point. Some people genuinely believe it, but very few people know how to act on it. Most organisations are more up to date and careful about their methods for looking after their machines and their finances than looking after their people. It is nothing but a deception to say that people are our most important asset, and then spend inadequate amounts on training and personnel procedures for selection, induction and career development. The biggest deceiver is the manager who says 'people are our most important asset', then makes hundreds of people redundant at the first economic downturn.

I have every confidence in you. If you really did have confidence it probably wouldn't occur to you to mention it. We only express this confidence about people we are concerned about. This is a code for: 'I need to give you some support and encouragement because I think you are faltering.' It's an alternative to helping the other person to face up to and to overcome his weaknesses. You are treating this other person like a child, unable to handle the reality of events. If you treat your subordinates like children, don't be surprised if they refuse to accept responsibility.

These forms of manipulation are not the work of the devil. They are habits that managers acquire as a way of dealing with people with whom they fear to be open. You pay a price for behaving like this. Every time you do this you shed a layer of integrity from your skin. Manipulation creates dependency and caution in those around us. When we shade reality and treat people like children or aliens, what we get is simply more negative politics. It is self-perpetuating. If you think you are guilty of some of these habits, then give them some thought. Obviously it is foolish to become unpolitical. But you win more allies and supporters to back you in the really important struggles if you are able to replace manipulation with a more honest and direct approach.

Whenever you can, try to:

- tell your subordinates where they really stand with you;
- tell senior management about difficulties, disappointments or doubts, as well as about the good news;
- tell the organisation about it, if you are in a situation which is deteriorating;
- let others know your position on controversial business issues, especially in meetings.

Remember that influence and power are partly based on trust. The leader who is predictable, consistent and who makes his position clear is trusted and looked up to. If you manipulate, you lose this trust.

SOME CULTURES MAKE DIRTY POLITICS INEVITABLE

Some of the managers I interviewed identified their organisations as places where devious politics were positively encouraged by the culture and rules of the company.

Rosie Harris had this comment to make:

It has been the rule for a long time at the Prudential that we don't sack people. The culture is changing now towards being able to do so, but traditionally we couldn't. The result of this culture is that you are forced to be manipulative if you need to get rid of someone who is incompetent. I have such a person working for me now and it's a real problem. He will have been given good appraisals in the past because it would have been against our culture to confront him. My only option now is to sideline him. I would much prefer openly to get rid of him. These politics are part of the baggage you take on when you get a senior job. You have got to become aware of how people see you, and your role in company politics.

The chief executive plays a significant part in determining the nature of the politics in a company. If the top man allows himself to be manipulated it fosters machiavellianism. It's up to him or her to set the tone. One manager reports that manipulative politics in his company are reinforced by the behaviour of the chief executive:

> He is manipulative. One of our important lines of business had been run by someone who was an ideas man rather than a people man. The chief executive wanted him out and engineered him out. This manager found out about his fate at a board meeting, through a casual remark made by the chief executive about the new holder of his job!

On the other hand, the company culture may be one in which negative policies cannot easily thrive. As Jim Davies says:

> Dirty politics doesn't work in Saatchis. We've got to trust each other. People who get involved in manipulative politics don't last. People do come in from other agencies with different cultures and try it on, but they don't succeed. We prefer also to be open with our clients, although with some of our clients you can't always be like that because of *their* cultures. But mostly our clients like us because we're frank and refreshing and our style is jokey and light-hearted. Our business is about relationships. We try to ensure that we enjoy our relationships with our clients.

Keith Manning says that the culture at Bull HN discourages people from going overboard with politics:

> TV dramas are very infrequent here. Politics are dangerous and can rebound on you. There are some characters in Bull who rely almost entirely on politics; they don't succeed. There is a tendency among bright, intuitive people to think, 'I'll influence these people to get my goal.' But they don't do the hard work of thinking it all through. So, in spite of the politicking, their project fails because of lack of careful thought. When it goes wrong it's obvious that it's their fault.

In some cases you will see the politics change in a company as it merges with new businesses who bring different cultures. Managers must be alert to these changes. You must always know what is going on, and be able to recognise what is happening around you. You've got to listen carefully and accurately, sift fact from fiction and spot the unstated aspiration behind the stated. Watch out for changes. Perhaps the new bits of the business operate in a much more competitive market than the rest of the company. It can be confusing when you've got different cultures dealing with each other; the traditional dealing with the new. You've got to recognise why people behave like they do and respond in what makes sense in their culture. New businesses have their own values and priorities. So you have to show them benefits in terms of what *they* see as important. At senior levels such cultures may clash unless new rules are set about how the divisions are to do business with each other.

KEEP YOUR INTEGRITY

Many of the managers interviewed felt very strongly that, although they had to get involved in politics, they would make sure to keep their integrity by avoiding dirty politics. Here is an excellent strategy for avoiding negative politics:

> If you want to make enemies of people – ignore them, give them the brush-off, ignore their egos. I try to see the good in people. I don't see my opponents as enemies, just as people who need more convincing. If they are not convinced, the fault is on my side. I try to work on my communication skills. When I do explain things properly and personally they usually come round. Few really want to stamp on you if you take this time and trouble with them.

Another strategy which doesn't involve you in negative politics is to disarm your enemies with openness. Give in on certain things when you can. You must give in sometimes in order to get what you want.

If you want to avoid losing out to negative politics, the answer is not to indulge in them yourself. Spend the time and effort in making friends and getting support for your ideas. Allies that you have made through contact building, and open, honest behaviour will usually back you up when you are in trouble. But you do need friends in high places when the going gets tough. Here is a sad story of a manager who lost out in a power battle because his opponent had more powerful support than he had:

> We were approached in my division to see if we would take on a teacher for a year as part of an exchange scheme. We agreed, and a bright woman

teacher in her thirties from a well-known London school was chosen. She worked directly for my boss David, the corporate development director.

I gave this teacher (Sally) as much help as possible, because it is difficult for a woman to do well in such a male-dominated industry. But I soon noticed, along with the rest of the office, that she was looking after her own interests very nicely already. My secretary intimated that Sally was having an affair with my boss David, but I didn't want to believe this. However, the evidence soon became overwhelming.

Sally and David were frequently seen working over reports in the wine bar in the evenings. I soon discovered that when David had to travel to the US, Sally found herself there at the same time. When we tried to contact her at one of the hotels on the schedule she left with her secretary we found that her travel plans were fictitious. More than once we called her at one of the hotels she was supposed to be staying at and were told that she wasn't staying there and wasn't expected.

Then the evidence began to get slightly sinister. Within weeks she had been given a company car, whereas the rest of us had had to wait the normal three years. She was given an unbelievable amount of responsibility, and it soon became clear that she knew all sorts of confidential things that she couldn't have known, unless David was telling her.

I didn't approve of the relationship as David was married, but I decided that it was none of my business so I kept quiet about it. But in the end I began to suffer as a result of their relationship. Within a year I found that I couldn't get to talk to David, he was always busy. He just froze me out. Increasingly he gave Sally work that I would normally do, especially if it meant that they could travel somewhere together. I was told that the managing director of a European branch didn't like my work, so Sally replaced me on that project as well. David even gave me poor performance appraisals which I didn't deserve.

Similar things were happening in the office to my other colleagues. They were being suppressed to facilitate Sally's ascent. So I decided to spill the beans. I spoke to personnel and to the chairman. Personnel would do nothing. The chairman, when faced with a denial from David, also refused to act. He was a weak man, and having recruited David himself originally, didn't want to be seen as having made a mistake.

In the end, even though everyone knew about David and Sally, no one would stand up to him. What David had, that the rest of us lacked, was a good solid power base. He had friends in all the right places. When the company was taken over recently the weak chairman only lasted six months. But David got a big job in the US through his influential friends in the new parent company. And he made sure that Sally got a good job in Paris. He totally abused his power, yet because his power base was so strong I could not unseat him, nor could I defend myself from his antics. I see now that without having powerful sponsors to back me up I didn't stand a chance against David. Finally, I felt that I could not live with the situation and decided to leave the company. I landed on my feet in an excellent job where conditions didn't favour such blatant abuse of power. I had to leave in order to protect my career and self-respect. The others who stayed and kept quiet are sorry now that they allowed this to happen without protesting, but they feared reprisals at the time.

It seems from this story as if the baddies got their way, and as if Sally's manipulative route to power through her lover was an effective one. Well, it was. But the story isn't over yet. Sally is in a risky position. Her only protector in the organisation is David. If anything happens to him she won't last a day. Everyone in the company knows the story. She did not get into a senior job through the normal route of high performance, experience and building alliances with a number of people. She only has one ally and is dependent on his continued success for her own.

In company politics it is not always the good who come out on top. But the people who do get on by manipulating and harming other people have a large number of enemies, and they never know when one of these enemies is going to stab them in the back. They also have the problem of living with themselves. If you don't mind living a life where a number of people despise and mistrust you, and you need eyes in the back of your head to watch the movements of your enemies, then you may choose to indulge in power plays and devious tactics. But it is a high-risk existence and nobody will pick you up when you fall.

If, on the other hand, you wish to maintain your integrity and behave in a constructive and positive way, then it is possible to do so without always losing out to the machiavellians. Remember the following:

- build a good network of contacts;
- get powerful sponsors early on in your career;
- empower your subordinates so that they help you to achieve results;
- negotiate with people instead of fighting with them;
- be aware of the politics around you and seek help in good time when you are in danger;
- gain power through strategic means rather than through manipulation.

If you use these constructive strategies, and combine them with high performance, you will have a more secure seat at the top *and* you will get there with a clear conscience.

REFERENCES

Key to Footnotes

1. Adapted from Stead, Bette Anne: *Women in Management*, Prentice Hall 1985.

2. Bryce, Lee: *The Influential Woman*, Piatkus 1989 and 1994.

3. Shea, Michael: *Influence*, Century Hutchinson, 1988.

4. Adapted from Sayles, Leonard R: *Managing in Real Organisations*, 2nd edn, McGraw Hill 1989.

5. Adapted from Ryan, Margaret: Manpower Services Commission training materials.

6. Adapted from Heaton, Ros and Berry, Susan: Independent Management and Training Consultants 1989.

7. Cunningham, Graham: Independent Management Consultants 1991.

8. Adapted from Butler, Pamela E: *Self Assertion for Women*, Harper and Row 1981.

9. Adapted from Shaw, Malcolm E: *Assertive Responsive Management*, Addison Wesley 1986.

10. Mintzberg, Henry: *The Nature of Managerial Work*, Harper and Row 1973.

11. Adapted from Handy, C: *Understanding Organisations*, 2nd edn, Penguin, 1985.

12. Adapted from Block, Peter: *The Empowered Manager*, Jossey-Bass 1991.

USEFUL ADDRESSES

COURSES AND CONSULTANCY

The Influential Manager

British Institute of Management
Management House
Cottingham Road
CORBY
Northants
NN17 1TT   Tel. (0536) 204222

For in-house courses, consultancy and individual counselling

The author's company:
Denham-Nash Ltd
22 Ailsa Road
St Margaret's
TWICKENHAM
Middlesex
TW1 1QW   Tel. 081-891 0033 and 081-892 7645

Image Consulting

Image consultancy for both men and women:
CMB (Colour Me Beautiful)
49 Greencoat Place
London
SW1P 1DS   Tel. 071-627 5211

RECOMMENDED READING

Argyle, Michael: *Bodily Communication*, Routledge 1990.

Back, K and K: *Assertiveness at Work*, McGraw Hill 1990.

Block, Peter: *The Empowered Manager*, Jossey-Bass 1991.

Bryce, Lee: *The Influential Woman*, Piatkus 1989 and 1994.

Harris, Amy and Thomas: *Staying OK*, Pan Books 1986.

Stuart, Christina: *Effective Speaking*, Pan Books 1988.

INDEX

action planning 58-9
  chart 59
action, ensuring meetings lead to 122
aggressive behaviour 139-40
  indirectly 140
  manipulation with indirect aggression 140
  short-term advantages of 139-40
alliances, building long-term 38-9, 62-3
allies in meetings 105
anger, dealing with 157-8
anxiety 41
appearance, personal 152
argument, power of 25
Arthur Guinness Son and Co 7
assertive behaviour 141-3
  advantages 141-2
  enhancing management skills 142-3
  guidelines for 143-4
  responsive 147-9
  techniques *see* assertiveness techniques
  your rights 144-5
assertiveness techniques 152-8
  dealing with anger 157-8
  dealing with manipulation 154-5
  discouraging and confronting passive behaviour 157
  making requests 153
  receiving criticism 156-7
  saying 'no' without feeling guilty 153-4
association, measuring your power from 73-4
authority and deference, earning 69
autocratic boss, influencing 100

bad boss, dealing with 100-2
Bahrain, Emir of 9
Bankers Trust 7, 82, 131
BBC Wildlife magazine 11
Beefeater 8, 70
beliefs and feelings, power of 145-6
benefits for your group, getting 68
'Big Bang' 7
Bodily Communication (Argyle) 152
body language 150-2, 179-81
  appearance 152
  breathing 152
  eyes 151
  gestures 152
  mouth 151
  posture and distance 151
  questionnaire 180
  speaking 152
  voice 151-2
Borg Warner case 129-30, 132, 136-7
boss, influencing your 88-103
  autocratic boss 100
  dealing with bad boss 100-2
  dealing with senior people 90-2
  don't get too close 102-3
  don't surprise boss 95-7
  emotional aspects 92
  getting rid of incompetent boss 102
  get to know your boss 97-9
  vs manipulation 88-90
  overcoming barriers to upward influence 94-7
  put yourself in boss's shoes 89-90
  saying 'no' to boss 99-100
  seeing from boss's angle 92-4

typical scenario 93-4
BP 8
breathing 152
British Airways 63
British Telecom 3-4, 48, 61, 84, 191, 194
broken record technique 154-5
Bull HN Ltd 6, 18, 187, 203
Burmah Castrol 9, 18

Castrol Ltd 9, 83, 98
chairing meetings 119-22
  control by using process 120-1
  don't dominate 121
  goals and assumptions 119
  ensure meeting leads to action 122
  structure 119-20
  timing 121
charisma, as influence style 50
Chemical Industry Training Board 14
Citibank 7, 36, 131
Citicorp International Bank Ltd 7
clarifying 107
clarity about what you want 56-61
clichés, avoidance of 116
colour and power dressing 177-8
communications
  lateral 182-4
  map 64
Condé Nast and National Magazines
  Distributors Ltd 11, 59-60, 82
coercion, as influence style 48-9
conforming without creeping 170-1
consensus 126-7
contacts, making *see* networks
content vs process 105-6
control
  over resources, power from 21
  by using process, in chairing meetings
   120-1
co-operation, getting 85-6
Coopers and Lybrand 4
Coopers Deloitte 4, 36, 189-90
Cornfield, Bernie 5
counterdependency in meetings 110-11
Courage brewers 10-11
Craven, John 7
credibility 42-3
  acquiring 66-7
critical areas 70-1
criticism
  giving 156-7
  handling 114-15, 156-7

receiving fair 156
  unfair 156
culture, organisational 78-9
Curry's 5

Davies, Jim 10, 24, 62-3, 198, 203
Dearden, Mike 8-9, 18, 19, 32, 42-3, 55,
  83, 97-8, 101, 117, 164, 170, 186
defeat, handling 160-3
  judging when decision is final 162-3
  when to make a fuss 163
  you often get another chance 164-5
deference, earning 69
delegating responsibility, ground rules for
  131-3
Deloitte, Haskins and Sells 4
Deloittes 9, 163, 170, 189
Deutsche Bank 7
developing ideas 108-9
developing personal power 138-58
  aggressive behaviour 139-40
  assertive behaviour 141-3
  assertiveness techniques 152-8
  body language 150-2
  inner voice: power of beliefs and feelings
   145-6
  passive behaviour 140-1
  softening your style 146-50
  take your people skills seriously 158
developing powerful image 169-81
  approachability 172-3
  awareness of fashion changes 171-3
  body language 179-81
  be true to yourself 173
  conform but don't creep 170-1
  less traditional organisation 178
  people who break the rules 178
  power dressing for men 174-6
  power dressing for women 176-8
  smart image builds confidence 171
direction, giving 68
Director, The 12
Directors Publications 11-12
dirty politics 193-207
  being strategic and instrumental in
   relationships 197
  creating monopolies to increase power
   194-5
  dropping people in it 197-8
  examples of 194-8
  inevitable in some cultures 202-4
  and keeping your integrity 204-7

manipulating facts to increase influence 195-6
manipulating people's emotions 196
manipulative negotiation 196-7
unintentional manipulation 198-202
Distillers 8
Dixons 5, 173
dominating in meetings 111
    avoidance of, in chairing 121
Dorland Advertising 10
dressing *see* power dressing
dropping people in it 197-8
Dyke, Greg 2-3, 22, 23, 197

Ealing Hospital 12, 13
education, as influence style 49
Effective Speaking (Stuart) 117
Elliott Automation 6
emotional aspects of dealing with boss 92
emotional problems in groups 109
    counterdependency 110-11
    dominating 111
    goals and needs 110
    identity 109-10
    intimacy 110
    pairing up 111
    power 110
    withdrawing 111
emotions, manipulating 196
emotive appeals, as influence style 49
empowering of others 123-37
    building in safeguards 137
    dangers and difficulties 135-7
    disadvantages 134-7
    establishing success criteria for team
        128-30
    to give rewards and incentives 134
    ground rules for delegating responsibility
        131-3
    partnership 130-1
    reasons for 124-6
    support 133-4
    team work 127-8
    techniques 126-34
encouraging 108
English Electric 6
European Cellars Ltd 13, 45-6
expertise
    influence style 50
    measuring 72-3
    power 22
    required in new job 82-3

eyes 151

failure, coping with (questionnaire) 166-8
    negative reactions 166-7
    positive reactions 167
false supportiveness 199
fashion changes, keeping aware of 171-3
Faunch, Rosie 12, 27-8, 84-5, 139, 142,
    155, 177
feelings and beliefs, power of 145-6
Fisons 14
Fitch Lovell 5
formal channels, influence through 33-4
French, Roger 4, 32, 36, 85, 125, 189-90

gatekeeping 108
gestures 152
getting in: starting to influence 40-3
    anxiety 41
    credibility 42-3
    influencing the right person 43
    personal gain or loss 41
    rapport 42
    trust 40-1
getting action 39, 43-53
    chart 44
    choosing influence strategy 45-7
    getting timing right 48
    influence styles 48-52
    planning ahead 43-5
    put yourself in other person's shoes 52-3
getting out: establishing genuine influence
    53-4
giving information 107
goals
    and assumptions, in chairing meetings
        119
    departmental differences in 185-7
    and needs, in meetings 110
    setting 57-61
group process 105-9
Guide Dogs for the Blind 13, 14, 40

hair 176
harmonising 108
Harris, Rosie 9, 19, 23, 36, 113, 118,
    133-4, 161-2, 163-4, 170, 193, 202
Harvard Business School 3
helping other people 67
Hobson Bayntun 5
Homes and Marchant 5
Honeywell 6

Hoskyns, Sir John 12
Hughes, Tony 7-8, 18, 23, 26, 49, 70, 82, 125, 134, 173, 186, 192

IBM 4
ICL 5, 6
ICT 6
identity in meetings 109-10
image
  consultants 176
  powerful *see* developing powerful image
  and trappings, power from 25-6
incompetent boss, getting rid of 102
indirectly aggressive behaviour 140
  manipulation with 140
influence
  choosing strategy 45-7
  defining 32-54
  don't rely on formal channels 33-4
  informal networks of 34-9
  how to use 32-3
  manipulating facts to increase 195-6
  and power 32-4
  skills to help us be influential 39
  styles 48-52
  see also influential behaviour; networks
    of influence
influencing other departments 182-92
  approaching the right people 191-2
  dealing with people you don't see every
    day 184-5
  differences in goals and values 185-7
  differing philosophies 187-8
  lateral communications 182-4
  through negotiation 188-90
  when negotiations fail, move up
    hierarchy 190-1
influencing the right person 43
influential behaviour 39-54
  getting action 39, 43-53
  getting in 39, 40-3
  getting out 39, 53-4
informal networks of influence 34-9
information
  giving 107
  power 23
  seeking 106
initiating 106
inner voice: power of beliefs and feelings
  145-6
innovation, measuring your power of 74
Institute of Directors 10, 12, 19

integrity, keeping your 204-7
interpersonal skills, measuring 74
intimacy in meetings 110
IOS 5

joint problem-solving, as influence style 51

Lainas, Michael 5, 78-9, 158, 173, 186-7,
  193
lateral communications 182-4
  cost of not devoting time to 183-4
London Programme, The 3
London Stock Exchange 7
London Weekend Television 3
long-term alliances, building 38-9
losing gracefully 159-68
  handling defeat 160-3
  how do you cope with failure? 166-8
  implementing unwanted decision 165-6
  turning defeat into victory 163-4

McKinsey 7
maintenance process 107-9
  developing ideas 108-9
  encouraging 108
  gatekeeping 108
  harmonising 108
make-up 178
making requests 153
management style 81
  empowerment and 126
manipulation 88-9
  dealing with 154-5
  of facts to increase influence 195-6
  with indirect aggression 140
  of people's emotions 196
  unintentional 198-202
manipulative negotiation 196-7
Manning, Keith 6, 18, 20, 31, 42, 85, 97,
  99, 122, 126-7, 134-5, 136, 170, 172,
  187, 203
Marketing Solutions 5, 78-9
Marks and Spencer 4
Mastercare 5
matrism and patrism 29-31
measuring your current power 72-5
  association 73-4
  expertise 72-3
  innovation 74
  interpersonal 74
  position power 72
  resource control 73

meetings, influencing at 104-22
  chairing 119-22
  developing process skills 111-17
  emotional problems in groups 109
  group process 105-9
  maintenance process 107-9
  make allies not enemies 105
  preparation 117-19
  task process 106-7
mentors 66
men, power dressing for 174-6
Middlesex Hospital 12
Mills, John 13-14, 40, 43, 84, 102, 124, 164-5
mistakes, power from owning up to 22
Mitsubishi Corporation 7
modelling, as influence style 50
monopolies to increase power, creating 194-5
Morgan Grenfell 7
mouth 151
Muirhead, Bill 10

name dropping 199
National Health Service 12, 27
negative politics *see* dirty politics
negotiation
  influence through 50
  manipulative 196-7
  with other departments 188-90
Nell, Tom 13, 18, 19-20, 25, 34, 41, 45-6, 112, 118, 125-6, 127-8, 165, 171-2, 184-5
networks of influence 34-9
  building long-term alliances 38-9
  how to build 35-7
  informal 34-9
  women and 36-7
  staying in 37-8
new job, establishing power in 76-87
  avoid early mistakes 83-4
  culture 78-9
  dealing with resistance 86-7
  expertise 82-3
  find out what you need to know 77-83
  get co-operation 85-6
  gain status gradually 84-5
  getting informed before starting 83
  management style 81
  people 81-2
  settling in 76-7
  values 79-81

new projects, starting 69-70
Nicholas, John 10-12, 19, 20-1, 22, 23, 59-60, 82
non-directive influence style 51

Orchestra of the Age of Enlightenment 7
organisational vs personal power 26-9
Ovaltine 10
overcoming barriers to upward influence 94-7
  don't surprise boss 95-7
  give the full truth 95
  keep an open mind 95
  weed out minor complaints 94
overselling 115
owning up to mistakes, power from 22

Packer, Kerry 197
PA Consulting Group 8, 79-81
pairing up in meetings 111
panic 77
partnership 130-1
passive behaviour 140-1
  discouraging and confronting 157
  as safe, low-risk option 141
patrism and matrism 29-31
personal gain or loss 41
personal power
  developing *see* developing personal power
  negative 26-8
  vs organisational power 26-9
  positive 28
personal relationships, importance of good 66
Philblack 8
philosophies, differing between departments 187-8
Phoenix Securities 7
planning ahead 43-5
Plesseys 5
politics *see* dirty politics
position power 20-1
  measuring 72
positive personal power 28
Post Office 3-4, 60-1, 65
posture and distance 151
power
  of argument 25
  from control over resources 21
  defining 15-31
  different views on 18-26

from doing unpleasant things 21-2
expert 22
from image and trappings 25-6
and influence 32-4
information 23
in meetings 110
negative personal 26-8
not a dirty word 15-17
from owning up to mistakes 22
patrism and matrism 29-31
personal vs organisational 26-9
position 20-1
positive personal power 28
referent 24
referred 24
responsibility of 29
of values 26
of vision 23
see also empowering of others
power dressing
  colour 177-8
  hair 176
  getting detail right 177
  image consultants 176
  make-up 178
  for men 174-6
  shirts 174
  shoes 176
  spectacles 175
  suits 174
  ties 175
  trousers 175
  for women 176-8
powerful, making yourself 55-75
  acquiring credibility 66-7
  clarity about what you want 56-61
  earning authority and deference 69
  getting benefits for your group 68
  getting sponsors and building alliances 62-6
  getting started from power base 61
  giving direction 68
  helping other people 67
  looking to top of organisation 55-6
  measuring your current power 72-5
  starting new projects 69-70
  strategies 75
  working in critical areas 70-1
powerlessness, feelings of 77
preparation for meetings 117-19
presentational skills 115-17
presenting bad news 113-14

process
  vs content 105-6
  control by using, in chairing meetings 120
  group 105-9
  maintenance 107
  task 106-7
process skills to influence meetings, developing 111-17
  create light not heat 115
  don't threaten 113
  handling criticism 114-15
  presentational skills 115-17
  presenting bad news 113-14
  watch where you sit 117
Prudential Assurance 9-10, 19, 36, 133, 162, 170, 202
pull strategy 46-7
push strategy 45-6

qualitative standards of success 129
quantitative standards of success 128

Rank Organisation 5
rational/logical argument, as influence style 49
referent power 24
referred power 24
relationships, being strategic and instrumental in 197
resistance, dealing with 86-7
resource control
  power from 21
  measuring 73
responsibility of power 29
responsive assertion 147-50
  guidelines for 149-50
  questionnaire 148-9
rewards and incentives, empowering others to give 134
Road Transport Industry Training Board 14
Robson Morrow 4
Rolls-Royce 14
Royal Navy 10
rule-breakers 178

Saab Motor Company 129
Saatchi and Saatchi 10, 24, 62-3, 198, 203
saying 'no'
  to your boss 99-100
  without feeling guilty 153-4

saying one thing and meaning another
199-202
Schweppes 10, 62-3
seating position in meetings 117
seeking information 106
selling, as influence style 49
senior people, dealing with 90-2
settling in to new job 76-7
shirts 174
shoes 176
Simonds, H and G 10
smart image, to build confidence 171
Smith, Martin 6-7, 20, 21, 36, 82, 101,
130-1
softening your style 146-50
responsive assertion 147-9
South Bedfordshire Health Authority 12
speaking 152
spectacles 175
sponsors 62-6
communications map 64
how to acquire 63-6
Stanneylands 8
Steetly 8
Stockbridge, Jerry 3, 48, 56, 60-1, 64-5,
83-4, 125, 160, 173, 190-1, 193
structuring meetings 119-20
Stuart, Christina 117
styles of influence 48-52
charisma 50
coercion 48-9
education 49
emotive 49-50
expert 50
joint problem-solving 51
modelling 50
negotiation 50-1
non-directive 51
rational/logical argument 49
selling 49
softening *see* softening your style
success criteria for team work 128-30
Borg Warner case 129-30
qualitative standards 129
quantitative standards 128
targets 129
suits 174

summarising 107
support, giving 133-4
supportiveness, false 199

targets 129
task process 106-7
clarifying 107
giving information 107
initiating 106
seeking information 106
summarising 107
team work
and empowerment 127-8
establishing success criteria 128-30
TGI Fridays 8, 49, 70, 134, 192
threatening, avoidance of 113
ties 175
timing 48
in chairing meetings 121
trailblazers 69-70
trousers 175
trust 40-1
TV-am 3, 197
TVS 3

unintentional manipulation 198-202
false supportiveness 199
name dropping 199
saying one thing and meaning another
199-202
unpleasant things, power from doing 21-2

values
company 79-81
departmental differences in 185-7
power of 26
table of 80
vision, power of 23-4
voice 151-2

Wandsworth Council 3
Whitbread Beer Co 7, 8, 13, 18, 23-4, 25,
26, 49, 70, 134, 192
withdrawing in meetings 111
women 36-7, 133-4
power dressing for 176-8

Business Books for Successful Managers

Piatkus Business Books have been created for busy executives and managers who need expert knowledge readily available in a clear and easy-to-follow format. Titles include:

Better Business Writing   Maryann Piotrowski

The Complete Book of Business Etiquette   Lynne Brennan and David Block

The Complete Time Management System   Christian H. Godefroy and John Clark

Confident Decision Making   J. Edward Russo and Paul J. H. Schoemaker

Dealing with Difficult People   Roberta Cava

The Energy Factor: How to Motivate Your Workforce   Art McNeil

Firing On All Cylinders   Jim Clemmer with Barry Sheehy

How to Implement Corporate Change   John Spencer and Adrian Pruss

The Influential Woman   Lee Bryce

Leadership Skills for Every Manager   Jim Clemmer and Art McNeil

Powerspeak: The Complete Guide to Public Speaking and Communication   Dorothy Leeds

The PowerTalk System: How to Communicate Effectively   Christian H. Godefroy and Stephanie Barrat

Presenting Yourself: A personal image guide for men   Mary Spillane

Presenting Yourself: A personal image guide for women   Mary Spillane

Problem Employees: How to improve their behaviour and their performance   Dr Peter Wylie and Dr Mardy Grothe

The Right Brain Manager   Dr Harry Alder

Smart Questions for Successful Managers: A new technique for effective communication   Dorothy Leeds

The Strategy of Meetings   George David Kieffer

For a free brochure with further information on our complete range of business titles, please write to:

Business Books Department
Piatkus Books
Freepost 7 (WD 4505)
London W1E 4EZ